GUIDE OF THE BELIEVER

Purification and Prayer in Islam

Guide of the Believer

Purification And Prayer in Islam

Mustafa Umar

GUIDE OF THE BELIEVER
PURIFICATION AND PRAYER IN ISLAM

First Edition

ISBN-13: 978-1480119109

ISBN-10: 1480119105

www.instituteofislam.com

Printed in the United States of America

In the Name of God

The Most Kind and Merciful

Contents

Transliteration Table

Arabic Consonants

Initial, unexpressed medial and final:

ء	ʾ	د	d	ض	ḍ	ك	k
ب	b	ذ	dh	ط	ṭ	ل	l
ت	t	ر	r	ظ	ẓ	م	m
ث	th	ز	z	ع	ʿ	ن	n
ج	j	س	s	غ	gh	هـ	h
ح	ḥ	ش	sh	ف	f	و	w
خ	kh	ص	ṣ	ق	q	ي	y

Vowels, diphthongs, etc.

Short:	ـَ	a	ـِ	i	ـُ	u
Long:	ـَا	ā	ـِي	ī	ـُو	ū
Diphthongs:			ـَوْ	aw		
			ـَيْ	ay		

Preface

I BEGIN BY PRAISING ALLAH, Who sent us guidance concerning how to live in this temporary world, Who guaranteed the preservation of His teachings through books, and Who gave us a code of conduct which possesses the ability to adapt and evolve so that it can be suitable for all times and places. I ask Him to bless the last messenger Muhammad[1] and all those who follow his example.

This book teaches you how to pray to your Lord. Every Muslim is required to worship Allah not only because He is worthy of such respect but also because it is part of our purpose in life. As soon as one believes in Allah and accepts that Muhammad was indeed the final messenger, the first thing one must do is learn how to pray. In the beginning, a new Muslim is only required to learn the basics of prayer since it is impossible to learn all the details overnight. However, as one advances along the path of Islam, one must learn the detailed rules and

1 Muslims usually insert the words "peace be on him" after mentioning any prophet. We will omit this in writing for the sake of fluency and assume the Muslim reader will insert this himself when reading. The same methodology has been followed by the great Imām Aḥmad ibn Ḥanbal [d. 241 A.H.].

regulations concerning the various aspects of purification and prayer.

The intention to write a book on the detailed rulings of prayer arose the moment I picked up a few books on the subject of Islamic law. The literature was extremely cryptic and impractical. It was difficult to understand and contained many theoretical issues that would rarely ever arise in my life, let alone the life of an average Muslim living in a modern urban society.

Muslim scholars penned books on Islamic law according to what they felt was most needed during their time. Some of these experts expounded every minute detail they could think of while others opted for such a high level of brevity that a textbook on Islamic law could rarely be understood without the aid of a teacher. The detailed books served as excellent references while the concise texts were excellent for memorization and teaching purposes. However, it is rare to find a book meant for the masses that can be read independently, at least to some degree.

My goal in writing this book is to fill the void that I see, since scholars of the past had different perceptions as to what was needed in their times. Today, many educated people learn new skills through instruction manuals that are clear and easy to understand. These books avoid unnecessary theory and mainly focus on what can be applied. Such instruction manuals have successfully equipped millions of people with knowledge and skills they would otherwise have remained ignorant of. Muslims must utilize such successful techniques of instruction to impart necessary religious knowledge to those seeking to learn the essentials of Islam. Until this occurs, many of Islam's essential practical teachings will remain inaccessible to most Muslims despite the apparent plethora of books available about the religion.

Much time passed before I could finally muster up the courage to write even a basic book on the subject of Islamic law because of the sensitive nature of the topic. Nonetheless, it is nothing but the dearth of readable material which has compelled me to undertake such a venture. So I have moved forward with my goal, despite the existence of many more qualified than me, only because I couldn't find any book that filled this void. I pray that Allah accepts this effort and counts the time I invested as being, at least somewhat, on par with the sacrifices made by great Muslim scholars like Abū Ḥanīfah [d. 150], Mālik [d. 179], Shāfiʿī [d. 204], and Aḥmad [d. 241] who codified the details and methods of Islamic Law to make it more accessible for future generations. Furthermore, I pray that people benefit and that my observation is not too far removed from reality.

I have worked on this book for eight years, on and off, revising and re-revising to determine the most efficient way of teaching this subject. In the end, I remind myself that success does not lie in the acceptance of created beings but in what Allah accepts from my effort. Furthermore, it is a fact that Allah has only granted absolute perfection to His own book, the Qur'ān; therefore, my success in this endeavor lies only with Allah and I ask Him to overlook my shortcomings and mistakes.

Mustafa Umar

Phoenix. August, 2012

Introduction

The Islamic Way of Life

ISLAM IS A COMPLETE way of life which provides guidance from Allah to His creation. That guidance consists of practical instructions concerning human behavior in both individual and social existence. No one can know, through their own reasoning, what is good and bad in every age. People change their minds about things everyday as well as throughout their life.

The comprehensive instruction provided by Allah is, in reality, a blessing and a mercy rather than a burden. It is similar to the instruction manual which accompanies a complex device teaching one the best way to maximize its use. Rather than playing around with the device and trying to figure out its capabilities and limitations, the designer, who knows how it functions, teaches how to use it. It should come as no surprise then, than no one knows how humans should function and act better than their Creator.

In fact, almost every human thought and action can broadly be classified according to Islamic teachings as either being recommended or disliked, with varying degrees of emphasis, thus potentially channeling every moment of a person's life through Divine guidance. The human intellect could never have fully discovered the perfect way to live life since it is inherently limited and prone to error. Therefore, it is a blessing from Allah that He taught humankind what it would not have been able to figure out on its own.

The teachings of Islam have broadly been classified by Muslim scholars into the following categories for learning purposes:

- Acts of Worship [*ʿibādāt*]: This category includes all teachings pertaining to purification, prayer, fasting, *zakāh* [charity], and *ḥajj* [pilgrimage]. These are classified as acts of worship because they occur between a person and his Lord, rather than between people.[2]

- Family Matters [*aḥwāl shakhṣiyyah*]: This category comprises issues pertaining to a family from its inception [through marriage/birth] to its termination [through divorce/death]. It includes all teachings relating to marriage, divorce, child custody, inheritance, etc.

- Economic Transactions [*muʿāmalāt*]: This category covers lawful and prohibited economic transactions, contracts, property ownership, etc.

- Politics and Governance [*aḥkām sulṭāniyyah*]: This includes all teachings pertaining to the relationship between a government and its people on the national level as well as between other governments on an international level. Within it, the penal code [*ḥudūd*] and rules pertaining to war and peace may also be classified.

2 Even though zakāh will affect other people, its performance is still classified as an act of worship since it is a one-way transaction done for the sake of Allah, unlike a loan which would be classified as a two-way transaction.

- Food and Clothing: This category includes the different types of foods eaten and clothes worn by people.

- Manners and Etiquettes [*akhlāq*]: This category includes the everyday moral teachings such as visiting the sick, smiling at people, taking care of guests, etc. Within it, the science of purifying the ego [*tazkiyah*] from harmful traits such as anger may also be included.

The detailed teachings of Islam are not meant solely for elite Muslim intellectuals. The basics in every category should be known to every Muslim who is capable of learning them, so that one can act upon those teachings.

All of the teachings of Islam, when considered together, are known as the *sharīʿah* [3], or Islamic law. *Fiqh* is another word which is commonly used synonymously with *sharīʿah*, even though it differs slightly.[4] Although 'Islamic law' is a poor substitute for rendering the meanings for the terms *sharīʿah* and *fiqh*, it has gained widespread acceptance and will be adopted throughout this book.

---

3 *Sharīʿah* may be translated formally as Islamic law or informally as the Islamic way of life.

4 *Fiqh* refers to the human attempt to understand the *sharīʿah*. This is similar to the way that the scientific method is the human attempt to understand the universe in which we live. The universe is what it is, but science may incorrectly observe and describe it every now and then. Therefore, in a nutshell, the *sharīʿah* is what Allah really intended, while *fiqh* is the human interpretation of what Allah probably intended. However, the term *fiqh* is often used synonymously with *sharīʿah* by many Muslims and there is nothing wrong with such a usage. That is because we must act according to what we understand of the *sharīʿah* in everyday life. So studying the science of *fiqh* means that one is learning the guidelines prescribed by Allah.

Methodology

THERE HAVE BEEN thousands of books written on the topic of purification and prayer, and it is probable this phenomenon will continue until the end of time. Each book serves a specific purpose and audience. Therefore, no one should claim that there is no need for another fresh attempt to benefit the Muslims of today. The present work is based on several sources and has many unique features that cause it to stand out from the rest.

DEFINED FOCUS

In the study of Islamic law, there are generally four elements to learn:

1. The ruling on a specific issue [i.e. how much of the head must be wiped when washing for prayer].

2. The evidence for the ruling [e.g. Qur'an, *ḥadīth*, analogy, consensus, etc.]

3. The legitimate differences of opinions on the issue [e.g. wipe the entire head, one-fourth, one-third, or only a few hairs]

4. The reason or wisdom behind the action [i.e. wiping the head is both a physical and symbolic act of purification in preparation for standing in front of one's Lord]

For the average Muslim, priority should be given to the ruling and the reason/wisdom. The former allows one to worship

Allah correctly while the latter helps one to understand what is being done and gain a deeper sense of spirituality. This book will confine itself to only these two aspects of Islamic law, because including evidences and differences of opinions may be ideal, but in the current fast-paced world where everyone's time seems to be severely limited, it would likely distract the reader from what is most essential.

Furthermore, teaching this subject directly from the Qur'an and Sunnah [5] by presenting a text and then extracting rulings from it may not be the best approach, although many people do believe that it should be taught this way. The benefit of such an approach would be that it instills confidence that what one is learning is coming directly from an Islamic text rather than being the whim of a self-appointed authority.[6] However, the downside to this approach is that it is less structured and fails to cover many issues which do not directly fall within the confines of the text. Another drawback is that most texts of the Qur'an and Sunnah usually cover several different topics in one phrase. Adopting this approach would either require a teacher to present a cut-out of a few words from a text, or would cause the student to have several questions in one's mind about the other topics covered in the text that are not necessarily relevant to the discussion at hand.

An individual's confidence in a scholar could be established more quickly by either viewing the instructor's credentials,

5 The Sunnah refers to the practice of the Prophet Muḥammad. This has been transmitted through eye witness reports known as *ḥadīths*. I will be using the terms Sunnah and *ḥadīth* almost synonymously for the sake of comprehension, even though there are significant differences between them.

6 In reality, many people utilize Islamic texts to justify their whims by quoting them out of context or without a proper interpretive methodology. One should be careful not to be fooled by such people.

or when in doubt, by simply testing the instructor with a few questions to make sure that person is knowledgeable about the subject. A person should not insist on seeing every proof and argument, although if done politely and with good intentions there would be no harm in it. This is similar to the way a patient would validate their doctor's advice, without requiring the medical practitioner to explain the scientific details behind every prescription presented.

PRACTICALITY

There are many rulings in the several treatises on Islamic law which were practical at one time or another but have now ceased to be important in the life of the average urban Muslim. Are you allowed to purify yourself with the water in a container that has been left over after a donkey has drunk from it? What do you do if a rat falls into your jug of clarified butter? How many camels must you own before you have to pay *zakāh* on them? Are you allowed to pray on top of the Kaʿbah?

Whether or not the answers to these questions are important first depends on whether they are even being asked in the first place.[7] For most urban Muslims, these issues would almost never arise in their lifetime. Therefore, the methodology used in this book is to only focus on issues that are likely to occur.

By emphasizing practicality over theory, this work may serve as a complete guide and reference book for those who

7 It must be kept in mind that scholars of Islamic law often attempted to answer every possible question that may arise and extend as many analogies as possible to their logical conclusions. Theoretically, this is a praiseworthy effort the way a mathematician attempts to provide a solution for every potential variable in an equation.

want to practice Islam in their daily lives. It will also serve as a comprehensive introduction to Islamic law for those who would like to specialize in the field.

BALANCING LEGALITY WITH SPIRITUALITY

The way of life prescribed by Islam is not merely a dry set of rules consisting only of commands and prohibitions. The subject of Islamic law tends to focus only on the legalistic aspects of actions and their consequences. Someone who fails to balance this legal instruction with proper doses of spirituality ends up becoming overly dry in their Islamic outlook. The Prophet hinted at the dangers involved with having such a mentality when he said, "It might be that a person who fasts gains nothing but thirst, and a person who prays at night gains nothing but fatigue."[8]

In order to draw a balance between the spiritual and legal aspects of an action, an explanation usually accompanies acts for the reader to understand the underlying meaning behind it. For example, washing oneself before the prayer is not described as entering a state of 'legal purity' or 'ritual purity', as many books of Islamic law describe it. It is much more than merely a legal state and that is explained in the text.

COMPREHENSIVE APPROACH

A Muslim must realize that there is a lot to learn in Islam. A basic primer on Islamic law may address over 12,500 issues.[9] An issue would consist of a relevant question pertain-

8 al-Dārimī, *al-Sunan*, classified by Ibn Ḥajar as sufficiently authentic [ḥasan].

9 Kiānī, Tahir Mahmood, *Mukhtasar al-Quduri*, xxxii.

ing to Islamic teachings such as: how much of the head must be wiped in wuḍū', must the limbs be washed in order, is it allowed to take a break while washing, etc. All of these issues may not be relevant for everyone, but they do arise for many people and it is important for a Muslim to be familiar with them.

A person will not be excused for not knowing how to live according to Islam. It must be emphasized that ignorance is not bliss and that one will be held accountable with Allah for not learning whatever was in one's capacity to learn.

METHODOLOGIES IN ISLAMIC LAW

Following a Legal School

Today, there are two popular approaches towards studying Islamic law that have resulted in some unnecessary disputation. The first approach is to teach the subject through one of the four popular schools of thought in Islamic Law: the Ḥanafī, Mālikī, Shāfiʿī, or Ḥambalī school. These schools are named after their founders who developed specific methods to interpret Islamic texts. There are many benefits of studying one of the schools in depth, especially for those who want to become experts in the subject. However, one of the drawbacks is that some proponents of this approach criticize anyone who attempts to follow an opinion from another school.[10] It is insisted that a person must choose any one school, and then strictly stick to it. A person is not supposed to ask any Muslim scholar about an issue unless that scholar also follows the same school as the questioner.

10 Sadly, this criticism is even made against people who opt for another opinion *within* the school itself. The reality is that none of these four schools are as monolithic as they are sometimes presented to be. There are several differences of opinion within each school.

The reason why studying one school became popular is because it was a systematic way to train scholars who were to specialize in Islamic law. Similar to the way modern law schools train aspiring lawyers and judges by studying past legal cases, Islamic seminaries applied a similar approach by training students to understand the judgments given by the scholars of a particular legal school. It became common for scholars to be labeled according to the school they specialized in while, in reality, they would differ from their school if they felt that the argument made by another school was stronger.[11] Most scholars had no issue with this approach. However, as the Muslim masses became more detached from Islam they became less inclined to follow the *sharīʿah* and began to go from scholar to scholar questioning one after another, hoping to find someone who might give them an answer that is in line with their whims. Some scholars who took note of this behavior decided to put an end to it by promoting the idea that it is forbidden to take an opinion outside of the school one claims to follow. Many people continue to misunderstand this decision and assume that anyone who opts for an opinion outside the school they associate with must be insincere towards the *sharīʿah*. Such a sweeping generalization fails to give people the benefit of the doubt and is best to avoid.

The second approach towards Islamic law is to ignore the intellectual heritage left by these four schools and directly look at the sources of Islam afresh. It is insisted that no one should follow the opinion of another without knowing the detailed proof behind the ruling. While there may be benefits to this approach, it is unreasonable to think that the average person

11 Several prominent scholars throughout history differed with their own school such as Abū Bakr Ibn al-ʿArabī, Ibn Rushd, al-Nawawī, al-ʿIzz ibnʿAbdussalām, Ibn Taymiyyah, al-Kamālibn al-Humām, ʿAbdul Ḥayy Laknawī, etc.

should have to know, or would even be able to understand, the detailed evidence behind each and every single minute issue in Islamic law.

A more balanced approach is to realize that a Muslim is obligated to ask a person who has a firm grounding in Islamic knowledge when one does not know something. It is preferred to ask the most knowledgeable person, but that is often impossible to determine. The average Muslim must use their best judgment [*ijtihād*] in determining who to ask the same way an expert scholar must use their best judgment [*ijtihād*] when giving an answer. Both of them, the average Muslim and the scholar, will be judged by Allah according to their effort and sincerity.

Once an answer is received, you should act according to that answer. It is not recommended to pose the same question to another scholar unless:

- You need more information and are unable to reach the first scholar.

- The answer itself appears strange or poorly researched. In that case, another scholar who appears more knowledgeable in that particular field should be consulted.

- The questioner has lost confidence in the person initially asked either due to the answer itself or because of other reasons. Remember to only ask those people whom you have confidence in and try to give them the benefit of the doubt.

The Optimal Method

In this book, a third approach will be followed. One school will be used as a base to build the structure and content of the book. From there, other opinions will be adopted when it seems that there is a good reason for doing so.[12] There should not be any major objection to this approach since all of the opinions adopted have been held by reliable and recognized Muslims scholars, are based on proper evidence and reasoning, and are not selected haphazardly based on whims.

If you were taught something different than what this book presents, you have the following options:

- You may abandon what you were taught before and follow what is in this book. This is highly recommended if the source of your prior knowledge was not very grounded in Islamic knowledge such as a relative or friend.

- You may retain what you were taught before when a teaching is different to what is in this book.[13]

General Rules and Exceptions

In order to facilitate learning and minimize differences of opinion, the categories which any action may fall into are five, as follows:

- Obligatory [*farḍ/wājib*]: If you omit this act without an excuse it will be counted as a sin. An example of this is performing the five prayers on time.

---

12 This work is based on the Ḥanafī school of Islamic law but opts for the opinion of another school when it appears that it is closer to representing Islamic law.

13 For example, if you were taught to pray the sunrise prayer in a different manner, you may continue to perform it as you do while learning other prayers that you may not have known how to perform such as the funeral prayer.

- Recommended [*sunnah/nafl*]: If you perform this act it will be counted as a good deed. If you omit it without excuse you will not incur any sin. An example of this is performing the sunrise prayer.

- Permissible [*mubāḥ*]: It is the same whether you perform this act or not. It will neither be counted as a good deed nor as a sin. An example of this is to itch oneself during the prayer.

- Disliked [*makrūh*]: If you avoid this act it might be counted as a good deed. If you perform it you will not incur sin. An example of this is to wash the left arm before the right when performing wuḍū'.

- Prohibited [*ḥarām*]: If you perform this act it will be counted as a sin. An example of this is praying without wuḍū'.

All actions may be classified into one of these five categories. If you are faced with some difficulty, or exceptional circumstance, you should ask a scholar concerning your situation since circumstances dictate exceptions in Islamic law [see Appendix 2].

Differences of Opinion in Islamic Law

REASONS FOR DIFFERENCES

ALL THE TEACHINGS of Islam are derived from two sources: the Qur'an and Sunnah. However, neither the Qur'an nor the Sunnah is a living person to whom one can ask a question and receive an answer. To properly be able to use them one must be fully conversant with their language, mode of expression, historical context, and other factors. One way to utilize these sources is to apply an analogy when there is no specific answer concerning a particular matter. For example, modern drugs are not explicitly mentioned in the Qur'an or Sunnah. However, since wine is prohibited in the Qur'an, because it intoxicates a person, any other drug that has a similar effect is also prohibited for the same reason.

The main reason for the differences in understanding is due to the fact that some texts of the Qur'an and Sunnah possess a degree of ambiguity that can be interpreted in various ways. Also, not every report about the Sunnah is authentic so differences may arise on whether to accept a prophetic report or not. It is due to these two factors of *clarity* and *authenticity* that differences of opinion must exist in at least some areas of Islamic law.

This does not mean that the essential teachings of Islam are ambiguous or lost. For example, the texts which instruct Muslims to pray daily, fast in the month of Ramaḍān, perform the Pilgrimage to Makkah, abstain from alcohol, avoid fornication, and not eat pork are completely unambiguous and authentically preserved. Therefore, the obligatory or prohibited nature of these acts leaves no room for any difference of opinion in these matters.

However, the details pertaining to the core teachings may contain some ambiguities which leaves them open to interpretation. An example of a verse in the Qur'an which is open to a difference of opinion is the one which instructs Muslims to wash themselves before praying. Part of this verse [Qur'an 5:6] tells Muslims to wipe their heads with water before praying, and this has been interpreted by Muslim scholars in different ways. Some scholars held that the entire head must be wiped over while others said that a minimum of one-third or one-fourth would suffice. Yet another group considered that the minimum is to wipe over just a few hairs while maintaining that it is recommended, but not required, to wipe the entire head. There are many reasons why scholars have differed on this issue. Some of them are:

1. The Arabic letter 'bā' which was used in the verse can imply that either part of the head needs to be wiped or may be used for linguistic-stylistic purposes, in which case the purport would be to wipe the entire head.

2. There are several prophetic reports that the Messenger of Allah always wiped over his entire head when he washed himself before prayer. However, this could be understood to mean that it is a highly recommended practice rather than a compulsory one.

3. There are reports that the Prophet wiped over only a part of his head and then wiped over his turban. These reports can imply different meanings and have varying levels of authenticity.

There are other arguments on this issue which have been presented by scholars, but discussing detailed evidence is beyond the scope of this book. It should be sufficient to understand why they differed and how complex each of their arguments must be for the positions they held.

THE LEGITIMACY AND WISDOM BEHIND DIFFERENCES

Allah chose to communicate his revelations through the medium of human language, which is naturally ambiguous at times. If He wanted, the Qur'an could have been a strictly literal and finely detailed text like a book on mathematics. However, in His infinite wisdom, he decided to reveal a text such as the Qur'an which is perfectly clear in the most fundamental aspects of the religion while some minor details might be vague and open to interpretation.

One of the wisdoms we can perceive behind such a decision is that it stimulates our intellect and reasoning ability. By working hard to try to arrive at a correct understanding of what Allah intended in the text, our intellect becomes sharper and more developed. The faculty of critical thinking is a very important life skill.

Another reason why Allah might have chosen to be brief in some verses is that the Qur'an remains more interesting and artistic. If the book was overly detailed and literal, like a book of law, it would be a very dry and boring piece to read, especially considering that Muslims recite parts of it every day in prayer.

It is also from Allah's wisdom and mercy that he allowed people to hold differences of opinion. The following incidents demonstrate Islam's stance on differences in understanding:

- A group of Muslims were on a journey together when, all of a sudden, a piece of rock fell from a mountain and hit one of them in the head. The man was badly injured so he bandaged his wound and they continued on their journey. The next morning, he discovered that he had a wet dream at night and now needed to take a bath before prayer. The man asked his fellow Muslims whether there was any exception to the rule for him since he was injured. They replied in the negative and insisted that he must take a bath and wash his head. When the man removed his bandage and poured water over his head, he fell down and died. After returning from their journey they told the Prophet what had happened. He was furious, and responded, "They killed him! Allah might kill them! If they don't know, why don't they ask? Asking is the cure for ignorance." Then he explained to them that the man didn't have to wash his head because of his injury.[14]

- Two Muslims were traveling through the desert and it was time for them to pray. They had no water with them, so they both performed tayammum [dry ablution] instead. Later, they found some water and there was still time left for that prayer. One of them repeated his prayer, believing that it was necessary to do so, while the other one did not. When they returned from their journey, they asked the Prophet about which one of them was correct in his understanding. He responded to the one who didn't repeat his prayer, "You have followed my teachings, and your prayer counts." Then he turned to the other one and said, "You get double the reward [since you prayed an extra prayer]." [15]

- The Prophet ordered his companions to set out for a military expedition and instructed them, "Do not pray the ʿAsr prayer until you reach Banū Qurayẓah [a village near Madīnah]." A group of them were delayed on the way and the time for the ʿAsr prayer was almost finished. Some of them decided not to pray until they arrived, taking the Prophet's words literally. Others from the group insisted: "We will pray. The Prophet didn't mean that we should skip the prayer." After they arrived, they informed the Prophet what had happened, and he didn't criticize either of them for what they did.[16]

The three incidents demonstrate that there is room in Islam for differences of opinion within certain bounds. Sometimes

14 Abū Dāwūd, *al-Sunan*, 1:93, #336.

15 Abū Dāwūd, *al-Sunan*, 1:93, #338.

16 Al-Bukhārī, *al-Ṣaḥīḥ*, 2:15, #946.

a person may be blatantly wrong in one's opinion, like the Muslims who insisted that the man wash his injured head. Another time one may wrongly assume that something is required when it is actually recommended, like the person who repeated his prayer after finding water. Yet another time, two different opinions may be right at the same time. In the end, there are two criteria that must be applied in order to determine whether an opinion is legitimate [i.e. accepted by Allah] or not: being sincere in attempting to arrive at what Allah and His Messenger intended and having a solid grounding in knowledge to interpret the sources correctly.

DEALING WITH DIFFERENCES IN SOCIETY

People deal with differences of opinion within their society in various ways. One extreme is for a person to assume that one's opinion is always right and to correct others whenever they do something different. Another equally extreme view is that of passive relativism where a person does not care what others are doing. The first view fails to take into consideration that there may be two equally valid opinions on an issue while the second fails to care that someone else is making a mistake. For a beginner, the following approach is best:

- If you see a Muslim doing something contrary to what you have learned, then you should investigate why that person is doing so.

- If it is determined that one is doing so out of ignorance, then you must correct that person.

- If it is determined that one is doing so because they learned something different from a legitimate source of

Islamic scholarship[17], then you should not correct them and be content that you have learned something new.

- If the difference happens to be in an issue that affects the community at large and is not limited to an act of personal piety, then the issue should be researched, referred to a qualified scholar, and discussed. Differences of opinion on issues that affect more people than the person holding that view [such as whether women should attend the mosque] are delicate and require a compromise to be made between individuals.

No one should be adamant about the opinion they hold to the point that they look down upon others. You might even change your opinion over time the way many of the greatest Muslim scholars altered their views on issues throughout their life. Those who are never willing to see things differently are most likely the ones being close-minded.

17 Defining exactly what a legitimate source of Islamic scholarship entails is beyond the scope of this book. The general rule is to always give people the benefit of the doubt.

Purification

AFTER ACCEPTING ISLAM, the first duty a Muslim must perform is prayer. Before praying, you must purify yourself before beginning that act of worship. Purification before prayer is similar to the way you would take a bath and make sure your clothes are clean before meeting an important dignitary. Allah is more deserving of such etiquette than any dignitary. There are also many hygienic advantages to regularly performing such cleaning.

Purification consists of two aspects:

- Symbolic Purity: This is when you wash certain parts of the body, or sometimes the whole body, before attempting to pray.

- Physical Purity: This is when you make sure that your body, clothes, and place of prayer are all clean from impure substances.

Wuḍū' [*Ablution*]

BEFORE PRAYING, you must wash certain parts of your body before standing in front of Allah. This is called wuḍū'. Not only does it clean the body but it also has the spiritual benefit of washing sins away. Rather than having to wash the whole body before prayer, Allah has made it easy for us to only wash those parts which are usually exposed to dust and dirt like the face, arms, head, and feet.

HOW TO PERFORM WUḌŪ'

Before Starting

- Make the intention and be conscious that you are purifying yourself according to Islamic teachings.
- Begin with the remembrance of Allah by saying [18]:

بِسْمِ اللّٰهِ الرَّحْمَٰنِ الرَّحِيمِ

bismillāhir raḥmānir raḥīm

I begin in the name of Allah

18 It is disliked to supplicate or mention Allah's name in a toilet area because it is a place of impurity. If you perform wuḍū' in such an area then you may either say it before entering or say it in your heart. If a sink is separated from a toilet through either a barrier or significant distance, the sink will not be considered as the toilet area.

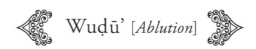

- Wash both hands to the wrists three times to make sure they are clean.

During

- Clean your teeth by brushing them, if possible. If you don't have a brush, you may use a wet finger instead. You may brush your teeth before beginning wuḍū'. If you didn't brush during wuḍū', you may do so before praying.

- Cup your right hand and fill it with water. Take that water into your mouth, swirl it around, and then spit it out. Do this three times.

- Cup your right hand again, fill it with water, and sniff it into your nose. Be careful not to hurt yourself by sniffing too quickly.[19] Clean the inside of your nose using your left hand and blow the water out. Do this three times.

- Cup both of your hands and fill them with water. Close your eyes, bring the water up, and wash your entire face. Do this three times.

- If you have a beard, comb through it with your wet fingers when washing the face.

- Wash your right arm from your fingertips all the way up to the elbow. Do this three times. Now do the same for your left arm three times.

- Wet both your hands and wipe over your entire head, beginning from the front and wiping to the back, and then returning to the front again.

19 Also, when fasting, make sure not to sniff too much or else you might end up swallowing some water.

- With the water left on your hands, insert your fingers into your ears and clean the inside with the index fingers and the back of your ears with the thumbs. If there is no water left, rewet your hands.
- Wash your right foot up to the ankle three times. Then wash your left foot three times. Make sure to get between the toes when washing.

After

- When the wuḍū' is complete, say the declaration of faith:

أَشْهَدُ أَنْ لَا إِلَهَ إِلَّا اللَّهُ وَحْدَهُ لَا شَرِيكَ لَهُ وَأَشْهَدُ أَنَّ مُحَمَّدًا عَبْدُهُ وَرَسُولُهُ

ash-hadu allā ilāha illallāh waḥdahū lā sharīka lah wa
ash-hadu anna muḥammadan ʿabduhu wa rasūluhu

I declare that there is no god but Allah alone, who has no partner, and that Muhammad is His servant and Messenger.

It is recommended to perform wuḍū' in this order and not to do anything else until it is completed. Make sure to use enough water to properly wash but do not waste water by being excessive.

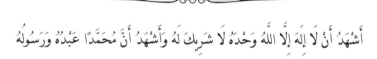

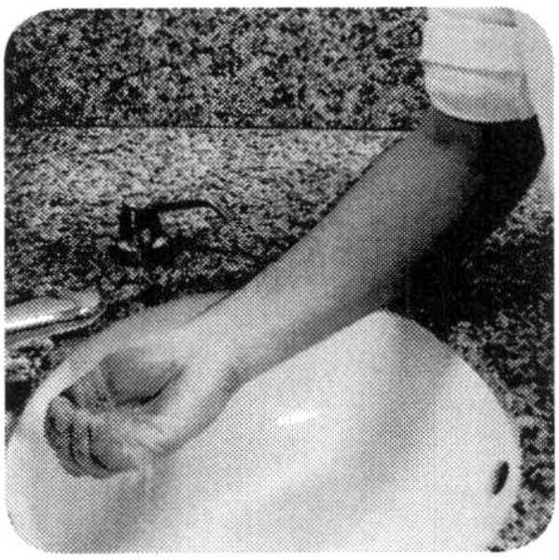

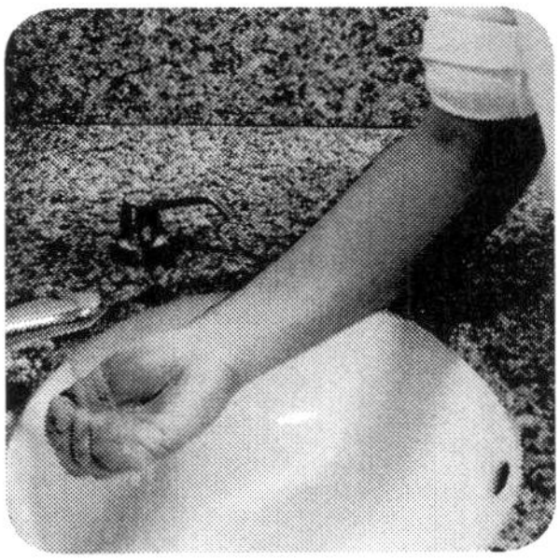

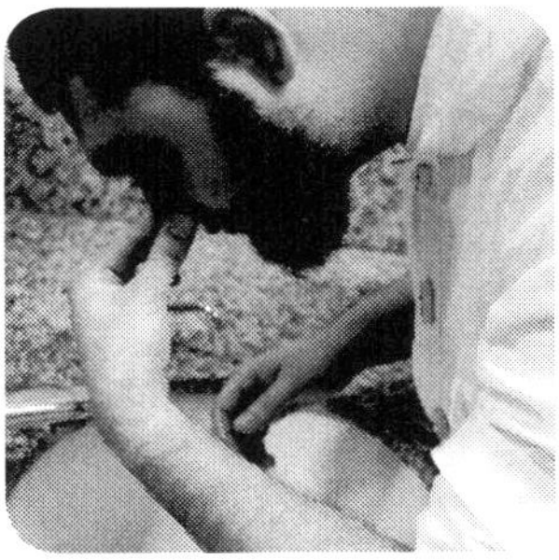

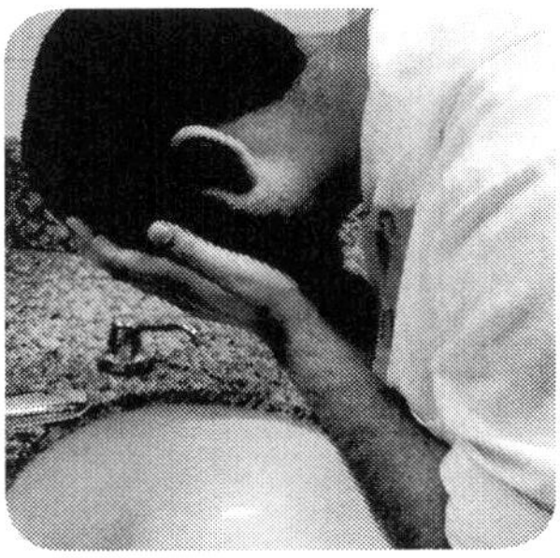

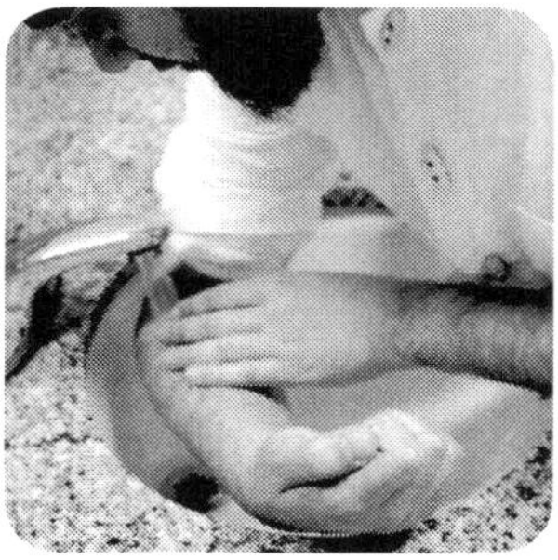

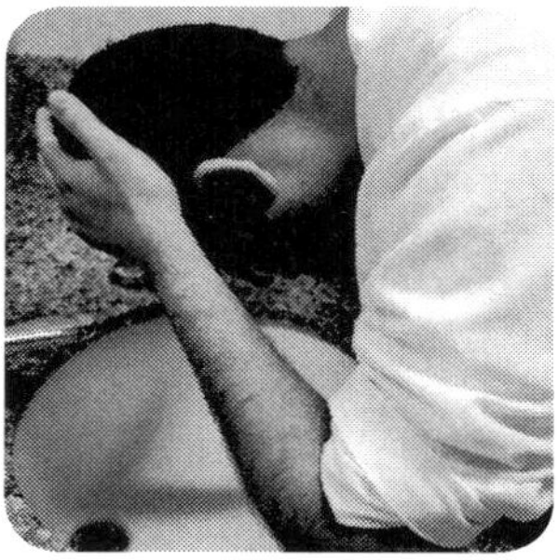

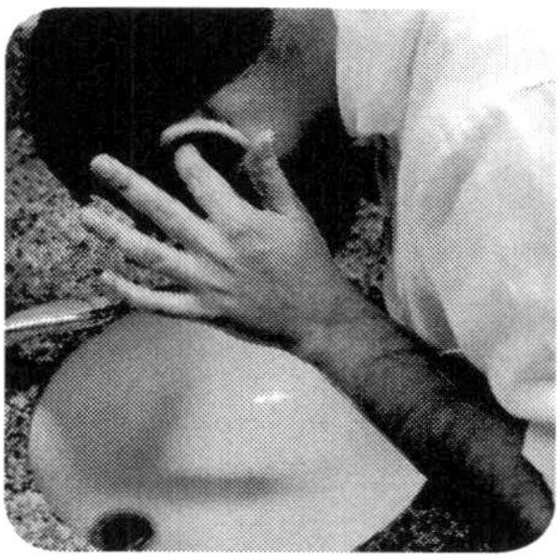

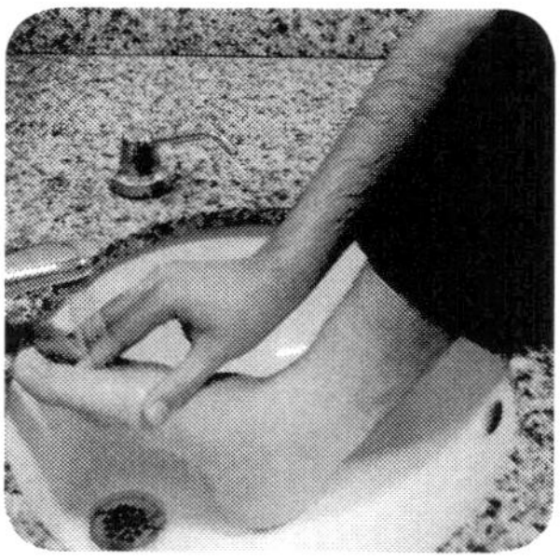

REQUIREMENTS

If any of the following is not washed completely, the wuḍū will not count:

- Washing the entire face, at least once, from the top of the forehead to the bottom of the chin, and from the beginning of one earlobe to the other. Thick facial hair, such as the eyebrows and beard, is considered to be part of the face so water does not need to reach the skin when washing.
- Washing each arm, at least once, up to and including the elbow.
- Wiping over at least part of the head with your hand. Women who find it difficult to take off their headscarf may reach under and wipe part of their head with their wet fingers. The minimum area that must be wiped is equivalent to at least three fingers of the wiping hand.
- Washing each foot, at least once, up to and including the ankle.

If anything prevents water from reaching one of these parts such as glue, paint, or nail polish[20], it must be removed before performing wuḍū'. Likewise, if you are wearing a tight ring or watch make sure water gets underneath to the skin when washing. Substances that do not form an insulating barrier such as ink, oil, lotion, and henna dye do not need to be

20 Breathable nail polish which does not form a watertight seal over the nails does not need to be removed during wuḍū'. A woman who would like to wear normal nail polish should do so during her period since she does not need to pray.

removed. Most of these places are usually washed three times to make sure no spot is missed.

LOSING WUḌŪ'

After performing wuḍū', you may perform any number of prayers until it is lost through one of the following acts:

- Having any substance come out of your private parts such as urine, stool, pre-seminal fluid, or semen. Normal vaginal discharge [i.e. cervical mucus] that is usually clear or white is an exception to this rule since it is a pure fluid and occurs regularly.

- Passing gas [flatulence] through the rear. However, the air that exits from a woman's vagina does not break wuḍū' since it is not a result of the digestion process.

- When either blood or pus exits the body in a large amount. However, if it is a small amount then it is overlooked.[21]

- When you vomit a mouthful such that you would not have been able to keep it in if you tried. However, if it is less than this, wuḍū' remains intact.

- When you lose consciousness either by sleeping, fainting, or through intoxication. However, if you sleep lightly in a position where you still have control over your body and can hear what is happening around you, then it does not break. This would happen if you were sleeping while standing or sitting on the floor upright. It would not break because there is little to no chance of you being able to pass gas.

21 This is according to the Ḥanbalī school. 'A small amount' is relative and should be determined according to your culture.

WHEN WUḌŪ' IS NEEDED

Wuḍū' is not only required for prayer but for other acts of worship as well such as touching a copy of the Qur'an. This does not apply to translations since the Qur'an is only in Arabic while a translation is merely an interpretation of the original's meaning. If there is a book which has a few verses of the Qur'an in it, it is fine to touch without wuḍū' as long as the amount of Qur'an in the book is less than the amount of non-Qur'anic material. However, the actual Arabic text of the Qur'an should not be touched out of respect unless one is in a state of purity. Taking this into consideration, a translation of the Qur'an accompanied by the Arabic original in one book is permissible to touch without wuḍū' because the introduction to the book usually makes the translation constitute more than half the book.

A portable device with Qur'an software is analogous to a book containing many pages [i.e. made up of several programs], therefore it is permissible to touch without wuḍū'. However, when the software is open, the Arabic text of the Qur'an should not be touched without being in a state of purity.

Bathing [*Ghusl*]

THERE ARE CIRCUMSTANCES where Allah has prescribed that wuḍū' is not sufficient to become pure. In that case you must wash the entire body by taking a complete bath [or shower].

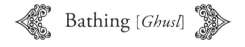

WHAT NECESSITATES IT

There are two instances when a Muslim, both male and female, must take a bath before prayer:

1. After ejaculation accompanied by sexual desire, whether this occurs during sleep or while awake.[22] If you take a bath and then more fluid comes out, you do not need to take another one since this was not accompanied by sexual desire and was a result of the previous desire. If you wake from sleep remembering an erotic dream, you only need to bathe if you find traces of ejaculatory fluid by observing its characteristics or smelling its odor.

2. After intercourse occurs. The bare minimum is for the male organ to enter the female.

If any of these two occur, the person is considered to be in a state of symbolic impurity, similar to when they are in need of wuḍū'.[23]

WHEN IT IS NEEDED

When a person is in need of a bath, the same acts which are not allowed without wuḍū' are also prohibited such as prayer and touching a copy of the Qur'an. However, in addition to these, it is also prohibited to:

---

22 Strangely enough, the existence of female ejaculation is a very controversial topic in Western societies and remains hotly debated in both the medical and social sciences. It may be rare, but does occur. A woman who reaches the state of orgasm must bathe before praying, whether or not something comes out.

23 Women also must bathe at the end of their period, which will be mentioned in a separate section on menstruation.

- Recite the Qur'an out loud. However, if someone is reading a translation of the Qur'an, quoting a verse in a lecture, or using the words for a supplication mentioned in the Qur'an, it is not considered recitation and is permissible.

- Enter the prayer area of a mosque without necessity.[24] Being present in any other part of the mosque compound is fine.

HOW TO PERFORM IT

Make the intention and begin with the remembrance of Allah as done in wuḍū'. Then start the bath by washing off any filth from your body and private parts, if there is any. It is recommended to perform wuḍū' during the bath as well. Then wash your entire body, making sure to clean the hard to reach places such as the navel, behind the ears, and under the arms. Also, make sure that water reaches the roots of the hair and beard. It is recommended to rinse the mouth and nose if you have not already done so in the wuḍū'.[25] Using soap or another cleansing substance is also recommended.

While it is necessary to wash [not wipe] your hair, there is one exception to the rule. If you [male[26] or female] have a complicated hairstyle [such as braided hair] which is quite difficult to redo, it does not need to be undone, as long as water flows over the hair and reaches the roots of the scalp. This is so that no one is overburdened due to their hairstyle.

24 The prayer area is designated through the intention of the people who design and operate the mosque. It does not refer to every place in the compound where people may actually pray.

25 This is according to the Shāfiʿī school.

26 This is according to the Shāfiʿī school.

If any part of the body is not washed properly, the bath will not count. So be careful when bathing.

Cleaning Off Impure Substances

IMPURE SUBSTANCES

THERE ARE MANY SUBSTANCES that people detest and prefer to avoid, and this varies from culture to culture. Islamic law has specified certain impure substances that must be cleaned off of one's body, clothes, and place of prayer before standing in front of Allah. Some things may be repulsive to many people such as sweat, saliva, and mucus, but these are deemed to be pure in the sense that they do not need to be cleaned off before one prays. Only the following things are considered impure:

- Anything which exits the private parts such as urine, stool, pre-seminal fluid, and semen. The urine and droppings of animals falls into the same category.[27] Normal vaginal discharge [i.e. cervical mucus] is considered pure since it is resembles sweat, saliva, and mucus more than it resembles an impurity.

- Vomit, blood, and pus.

- Intoxicating beverages. The prohibition against liquor is so strong that a Muslim should not even come into con-

27 According to the Mālikī school, neither the body, moisture, or saliva of a dog is impure.

tact with it. However, any form of alcohol that is prepared for medical or cosmetic purposes is considered pure.

If a person has a small amount of impurity on their body or clothes it is overlooked. A small quantity might be defined as a stain about an inch and a half in diameter.

HOW TO CLEAN OFF IMPURITY

Impure substances must be cleaned off before one can pray. This may be done according to one's custom and by using common sense. Here are some guidelines to make things easier.

If an impurity has afflicted an absorbent material such as a garment, it must be washed out with water. If the stain is visible, that area is washed. If it is not visible, wash the entire area the impurity might have fallen in and squeeze the water out. If a stain [such as blood] remains after washing with water, there is no need to use hot water or a cleansing agent, although it is better to do so.

If a substance is nonporous such as metal or wood, the impure substance may be wiped off and does not need to be washed. The same ruling applies to shoes and sandals that have stepped in urine or dung. If there is urine on the ground, it is considered pure after it dries out. If a baby urinates or vomits on a carpet that is difficult to wash, you may wipe off the impurity, pour water over the carpet, and either soak it up with a towel or let it dry out.

Impurities are only transferred from one substance to another if the area is moist. If it is dry, do not be so concerned that it will transfer and make your clothes or body impure by coming into contact with it. For example, if someone places a prayer carpet on a ground afflicted with dried urine, the carpet will not become impure. If the carpet was moist, it would only be considered impure if the color or smell of it had changed.

Impure substances which are very common in society and difficult to avoid are overlooked to prevent hardship such as street mud [containing impurities], traces of dried feces after cleaning yourself, etc. Remember that small amounts of impurity are overlooked as well.

Toilet Manners

AFTER RELIEVING YOURSELF, it is important to properly clean the private parts. This is not only hygienic but has spiritual implications as well, since being in a pure state is a prerequisite for prayer. The following etiquette should be observed when visiting the toilet:

- Relieve yourself in a secluded area so that no one can see you. Using an uncovered public urinal is against the etiquette of Islam.

- Do not take anything with the name of Allah into the toilet area unless it is concealed [i.e. in your pocket] or unless there is no safe place to leave it outside.

- Do not relieve yourself in any way or place that would harm you or others. For example, defecating on a mountain trail, on a wall, in an alley, or leaving drops of urine on the seat or ground is strictly forbidden.

- Do not urinate in a way or place where drops might splash back on you such as on a wall, unless it is necessary because no other place can be found.

- When outdoors, do not face the direction of Makkah nor turn your back towards it, out of respect.[28]

- Before entering the toilet area, say:

اللَّهُمَّ إِنِّي أَعُوذُ بِكَ مِنَ الْخُبُثِ وَالْخَبَائِثِ

allāhumma innī aʿūdhu bika minal khubuthi wal khabā'ith

Allah, I seek refuge in you from impurity and impure substances.

- Enter the toilet area with your left foot, since it is a place where impurity is disposed of. Places of purity, like the mosque, should be entered with the right foot first.

- It is recommended to sit whenever possible since this is more concealing and less likely to splash back.

- It is disliked to speak when relieving yourself, unless necessary.

- You must remove the impurity left on your body. Use your left hand to clean yourself either with water or a solid object [or both] after you finish. If water is used, pour it with a container using the right hand and then use the left

28 This is according to the Shāfiʿī school.

hand to clean off the urine or stool.[29] If water is not available, use a solid object such as toilet paper by wiping the area an odd number of times [as much as needed]. However, using water is preferred, since it cleans the area better.

- Exit the toilet area with your right foot, the opposite way you entered.

- After exiting, say:

غُفْرَانَكَ

ghufrānak

I seek your forgiveness.

- Wash your hands, preferably with a purifying substance such as soap.

Purifying Water

THE WATER USED for purification should be in its natural state. People gather water from many different sources such

29 There is nothing unhygienic in such a practice since the hand will be washed afterwards.

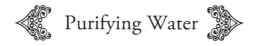

as rain, melted snow, rivers, and lakes. As long as the water is in its natural state, whether it is sweet or salty, it may be used for purification.

These are some other guidelines pertaining to water:

- If the water has been mixed with something else like perfume or chlorine, it is fine to use as long as it is still considered water and not another substance like tea [which is made from water but is given a different name].
- If an impurity has fallen into the water, it may not be used if the taste, smell, or color of the water has changed.[30]
- Used water that has been purified through a cleansing process is fine to use if the impurities have been removed.
- It is disliked to use something that may harm you such as recycled water which may potentially be dangerous.

Concessions in Purification

ALLAH DID NOT PRESCRIBE purification to make life difficult for people, but to make sure they are in a state of purity. There are times when it can be difficult to perform purification such as when traveling, during illness, in extreme weather conditions, etc. Therefore, if the requirements are met, the following concessions may be utilized so that purification is not overburdening.

30 According to the Mālikī school.

WIPING OVER SOCKS

Washing the feet during wuḍū' can sometimes be difficult, especially in cold weather or when traveling. Therefore, it is allowed to wipe over your socks as a symbolic substitute for washing the feet. It is from the mercy of Allah that this is allowed under all circumstances as long as some conditions are met.

How to Wipe

In order to take advantage of this concession, perform wuḍū' and put on your socks. When you lose wuḍū', your socks act like a barrier to prevent impurity from reaching your feet. When you perform wuḍū', do it as usual until it is time to wash the feet. Instead of taking your socks off, wet both your hands. Place the fingers of your right hand over the upper surface of your right sock near the toes. Wipe over the sock by moving your hand in the direction of your shin. Use the left hand to wipe the left sock in the same manner. The area that will be wiped over is the top part of the foot which is normally washed in wuḍū'. The minimum area that must be wiped is equivalent to three fingers of the wiping hand.

Prerequisites for Wiping

In order to wipe over your socks, these conditions must be met:

- The socks must be worn after being in a state of purity through wuḍū' or after taking a bath.

- The socks should be made of thick material such as cotton, wool, or leather such that water does not completely seep through to the foot when wiping over them. This does not mean that they must be waterproof. Also, they should not be so thin that they are transparent.

- The socks must cover the entire foot and ankle, since that is the area which is washed in wuḍū. If there are a few holes in the sock, that is overlooked. Wearing something that fulfills the same requirements as socks, like boots which cover the ankles, may also be wiped over.

- The period of time to wipe over socks is limited. It is allowed for 24 hours from the time you lose wuḍū', not from the time the socks are worn. After the time expires, you must take off the socks and make wuḍū' again. If a person is on a journey [31] then the period is 72 hours. If one begins wearing the socks and then later sets out on a journey, or vice versa, the time limit is based on the current state [i.e. if you set out on a journey you have 72 hours, but if you return from a trip the time is reduced to 24 hours].

Nullification of Wiping

After wearing your socks in a state of purity, the following invalidate your ability to wipe over them:

- If either of the socks is taken off [more than halfway].[32]

- If the time limit expires.

- If you are in need of a bath.

31 There are specific requirements for a person to be considered on a journey, which is covered in the chapter on prayer.

32 If you wipe over your boots and then remove them, the wiping is nullified even if you are wearing socks. However, if you wipe over the socks and then remove the boots while leaving the socks on, it is fine. The general rule is that whatever was wiped over must not be taken off.

If already in a state of wuḍū' when wiping is nullified you may take off your socks, wash your feet, and put them back on. This will start a new time period since your other limbs were already in a state of purity. Otherwise, you must perform wuḍū' again and repeat the process.

WIPING OVER AN INJURY OR BANDAGE

If unable to wash a certain part of the body due to an injury [or some other reason], the area may be wiped over with water instead of washed. If wiping would also cause harm, the injured area may be skipped completely.

If there is a bandage or cast on a certain part of the body which would cause difficulty if it had to be removed every time for purification, the bandage material is wiped over with water and that serves as a symbolic substitute for washing. At least half of it must be wiped over for this concession to apply.

TAYAMMUM [DRY ABLUTION]

There are times when it is very difficult, or even impossible, to perform wuḍū' or take a bath. This would occur due to a lack of water or an inability to use it. Therefore, there is a symbolic substitute which does not require water. It gives the believer a feeling of purity and demonstrates one's sincerity through the effort put in.

How to Perform It

Before Starting

- Make the intention and begin with the remembrance of Allah as done in wuḍū'.

During

- Place both hands [palms down] on the dirt and lift them up. You may blow or shake off some of the excess, but don't clean your hands completely.

- Wipe your entire face like you would for wuḍū'.

- Place your hands on the dirt again and wipe your right arm with your left hand and your left arm with your right hand, as you would for wuḍū'.

After

- Say the declaration of faith as done after wuḍū'.

Prerequisites for Tayammum

In order to be eligible to perform tayammum the following conditions must be met:

- You must not be able to find a sufficient amount of water to purify yourself. This usually only occurs when a person is traveling outside a city. Water that is needed for other purposes like drinking water while hiking does not need to be used. If there is a possibility that water is nearby [i.e. a few minutes distance], you must go search for it, and even purchase it if it is for sale. If you are confident that you will find sufficient water before the end of the prayer time, it is better to wait.[33]

33 It is also allowed to perform tayammum for the 'Īd prayer and the Funeral prayer if there is no time to perform wuḍū'. This is because these two prayers must be prayed in a group and once they are over, they cannot be made up.

- You must not be able to use water either because it will make you ill or prolong an illness you already have. If the water is very cold [34] and you can find something to heat it, you must do so. Also, if you are not able to find a private place to bathe, such as on an airplane, or while at work, you may perform tayammum.

- Only substances from the natural surface of the earth may be used as a substitute for water such as dust [35], dirt, rock, sand, marble, or clay. One way to tell whether it is from the earth's surface is that it will not burn to ash or melt when exposed to fire like tress, grass, and metals would. If a substance is painted over or glazed, it may not be used. Likewise, if it has an impurity on it such as blood or urine, it may not be used.

Nullification of Tayammum

Tayammum is a full substitute for wuḍū' and bathing. You can pray as many prayers as you like by performing it once. The following will invalidate your tayammum:

- Anything which breaks your wuḍū' or requires you to take a bath. In this case, you may perform tayammum again.

- When your excuse goes away and you find water or are able to use it again. In this case, your tayammum is broken, even if you are in the middle of prayer. You also return to the previous state you were in before performing

34 It must be cold enough to cause illness, not mere discomfort.

35 This refers to atmospheric dust found in nature and not domestic dust which is found in modern homes and buildings. Domestic dust is primarily composed of non-atmospheric elements such as human skin cells, hair, textile fibers, and paper fibers.

tayammum. So if you were in need of a bath, you must bathe, because tayammum was only a substitute but didn't actually purify you.

CHRONICALLY LOSING WUḌŪ'

When one is unable to maintain wuḍū' due to a chronic illness such as a recurring nosebleed, frequent leakage of urine, or abnormal vaginal discharge [outside of menstruation] there is a concession. Wuḍū' will not break due to that reason as long you are quite confident this problem will last until the end of the prayer time. If sitting or lying down will prevent this problem from occurring, you must do so and pray that way.

If this is the first time you are experiencing it, it is better to delay your prayer until the end of its time. The wuḍū' will break due to other reasons not connected with the problem. Also, one only needs to clean the impurity off their clothes once when performing wuḍū' because this is a constant problem which causes difficulty.

For example, a person with a recurring nosebleed should determine whether this condition will last until the end of the prayer time period. It does not mean that blood must constantly come out, but rather that blood comes out at least once unexpectedly during the prayer's time period. In this case, the person will perform wuḍū' and may pray. If the nose bleeds before or during the prayer, it is to be disregarded since it will not break the wuḍū'. When the time for prayer ends, the wuḍū' is broken. Through this method, a person with a chronic problem will make only one wuḍū' for every prayer period and will be considered to be in a state of purity until the end of the prayer time.

Menstruation & Lochia [*Postpartum Discharge*]

THE MENSTRUAL CYCLE is a function designed by Allah which prepares a woman for the possibility of pregnancy each month. This facilitates reproduction and the survival of the human race. An egg travels to the uterus which builds up a lining that consists of extra blood and tissue. If the egg is not fertilized the lining is not needed and is shed through the vaginal canal. This results in bleeding and discharge from a woman's body. The blood shed is usually between two to eight tablespoons per period.

Another function planned by Allah is that after childbirth a woman may experience vaginal bleeding and discharge. This is known as lochia and usually lasts for a few weeks. Lochia resembles menstruation and therefore follows the same rules in Islamic law.

WHAT IS PROHIBITED

Since a woman regularly bleeds during these periods there are some restrictions Islam has set to protect her and make her life easy. While experiencing her period she must refrain from:

- Touching or reciting the Qur'an. However, if it is very important for her to recite because she is a Qur'an teacher or she fears that she would forget what she has memorized then it is fine for her to do so.[36]

- Praying. She does not need to make up the prayers she has missed because this would amount to several every

36 This is according to the Mālikī school.

month. It is recommended that she take some time out of the day during prayer times to remember Allah, and perform other acts of worship.

- Fasting. She must make up the necessary fasts that she has missed because Ramaḍān only comes once a year and it is not very difficult to make these up.
- Entering the prayer area of a mosque without a good reason. Standing in any other part of the mosque compound is fine. Women who would like to attend classes or gatherings that are only being held in the mosque area may do so.[37]
- Having intercourse. She may engage in all other forms of foreplay as long as it does not involve her bare private parts and does not lead to intercourse. If her genitals are covered with a cloth then it is fine.

DETERMINING THE PERIOD

It is very important to precisely determine the beginning and end of menstrual bleeding and lochia because this will decide whether a woman should pray or not [or refrain from other actions].[38] Women who have a regular cycle usually know how to determine the duration of their period without any extra help.

When a woman notices her first discharge she should refrain from prayer and the other prohibited acts. If the time for one of the prayers has entered and she has not yet prayed, she is excused from having to perform it. When she believes her period

37 This is the opinion of al-Muzanī [of the Shāfiʿī school] and Ibn Ḥazm.

38 Precisely determining a woman's period has many functions in Islamic law related to purification, prayer, fasting, Pilgrimage [ḥajj], marriage, and divorce. This section will only deal with the details related to purification and prayer.

is about to end she should begin checking to see if it is over by either observing a white/clear fluid discharge or by inserting a piece of cotton [or other material] and making sure it does not come out stained by any colored discharge. Once she is certain her period has ended she must take a bath and resume praying. Now she will be in a state of purity again and all the prohibitions are lifted. If she cannot find a place to bathe, she may perform tayammum.

The age at which a girl begins her first period can vary greatly from person to person. It may be as early as eight years or as late as sixteen. She should be taught by a teacher or parent that it will be coming soon so she can lookout for it and report it to an adult. When it begins she should keep track of it on a calendar by marking the first and last day she saw blood. This will help her track when it will come next and how long it will likely last.

The menstrual period in a woman usually stops around the age of fifty, but can vary greatly from person to person. It means that she is no longer ovulating [producing eggs] and therefore cannot become pregnant anymore.

ABNORMAL UTERINE BLEEDING AND DISCHARGE

Most women experience some form of abnormal bleeding or discharge at least once in their life. According to Islamic law, abnormal bleeding and discharge is defined as any flow that occurs outside the menstrual or lochia period. If a woman bleeds or has discharge outside of her normal period, she does not need to refrain from any activities and is allowed to pray, fast, and have sex because this blood/discharge is different. She is considered to be in the same category as a person who chronically loses her wuḍū' [like a continuous nosebleed] and must perform it for every prayer time period.

The first few years of menstruation and the last few before menopause may result in irregular cycles, or even skipped periods. There are many other factors such as hormonal changes and stress which can cause abnormal periods or result in bleeding outside of a woman's period. Often times abnormal bleeding may occur directly before or after a woman's period which makes it very difficult to differentiate between what is normal and abnormal.[39] If it is not differentiated correctly it may result in a woman praying when she was not supposed to or skipping a prayer when she was obligated to pray. However, Allah does not burden people with having to consult a medical practitioner every time there is a doubt.[40] Women should use their best judgment and abide by the following guidelines to determine whether or not their bleeding is from a regular period or abnormal.

- If a woman has a regular period, she should consider any extra days as abnormal bleeding. However, if she is knowledgeable in distinguishing between the different types of blood and believes this to be part of the menstrual period she may consider it to be so.[41]

- If a woman sees some blood/discharge after taking a bath and she has a cycle that varies a little, she should try to determine what her 'normal cycle' is and then assume that any extra blood is abnormal. This is because, when in doubt, it is better to pray assuming that one's bleeding is

39 This is why Muslim scholars have differed so much in trying to set precise rules to differentiate between the two types of blood. See Ibn Rushd, *Bidāyah al-Mujtahid*, 1:55-62 and Ibn Taymiyyah, *Majmū' Fatāwā*, 21:630 for a detailed explanation on how and why they differed.

40 The truth of the matter is that even medical science is unable to precisely define what is normal and irregular.

41 This is according to the Mālikī school.

abnormal.[42] The 'normal cycle' should be considered as a duration that has appeared at least twice during the most recent periods.[43]

- If she has forgotten how many days her period lasts and cannot calculate her 'normal cycle', she should estimate it at being what the women from her culture and in her area generally have.[44]

- If lochia exceeds forty days it is automatically considered to be over and the discharge seen after the 40th day is deemed to be abnormal.

- Any spotting, discharge, or bleeding is considered to be abnormal if it occurs:

  - Before a woman has started menstruating.

  - After menopause.

  - During pregnancy.

  - Between two periods such that she is certain her first period has ended and the second has not begun. Any spotting or colored discharge during the period is considered part of the period.

Remember, the general rule is that if a woman is experiencing menstrual bleeding or lochia, she must not pray. If she is experiencing abnormal bleeding or discharge she must pray. When in doubt, it is better to pray.

---

42 However, in other issues pertaining to divorce and remarriage, it is better to wait and consider the blood as menstrual.

43 For example, if her previous periods lasted five, six, seven, and six days, respectively, her 'normal period' is considered to be six days. This is one of the opinion's within the Ḥanafī school.

44 This is according to the Mālikī school.

Prayer

PRAYER IS A SPECIFIC form of worship which Allah has taught His servants to perform. It brings one closer to Him and keeps one away from immoral conduct. It also purifies sins, the way a person is purified from dirt by bathing. The daily prayers are such an essential part of being a Muslim that it is one of the main factors which differentiates a Muslim who takes the religion seriously from one who does not.

Even one who does not completely understand the full meaning and import of prayer still benefits by taking time out of their day to stand in front of Allah. This, at minimum, demonstrates their dedication to Allah and clarifies their priorities in life. Furthermore, even a person who only performs the actions and recites the supplication formulas also displays some obedience to Allah. This is because they could have skipped the prayer, or intentionally made mistakes in it, but they chose not do so knowing that Allah is aware of everything.

The Five Daily Prayers

THE MOST IMPORTANT prayers are the daily ones which are prescribed five times a day. They refresh a person's belief in Allah and remind one concerning the true purpose of life. They are spread throughout the day so that people strike a balance between focusing on this world and the next. The prayers keep a person from getting too caught up in their work and in the materialism of this life.

WHO MUST PRAY

These daily prayers must be performed by all Muslims who meet the following conditions:

- Maturity: One is only held responsible for their actions in the sight of Allah after one has attained maturity and the intellect has developed.[45] This occurs during when a child reaches puberty. A boy is considered to be a mature adult when he has his first wet dream [or equivalent]. A girl is considered to be mature when she either has her first wet dream [or equivalent] or begins her menstrual period. If neither of these occur before the age of fifteen[46] they are considered to be mature at that age. Children should be taught how to pray by the age of seven and their parents must make sure they are praying by the age of ten.

---

45 The exact time when this happens is only known to Allah. However, we must approximate when this occurs for legal reasons to distinguish between a child and an adult, hence the following criteria specified in Islamic law.

46 This is calculated in lunar years according to Islamic law.

- Sanity: Those people who are afflicted with an illness or defect that impairs their intellect are not considered responsible adults. They are treated like children in that they are not responsible for their actions in this world or the next. However, they may still be taught how to pray and encouraged to do so.

THE FIVE PRAYERS AND THEIR TIMINGS

Prayer has been fixed at certain times spread throughout the day so that one is constantly remembering Allah. Prayer timings depend on the position of the sun so they change every day and vary from place to place. Each period lasts a certain amount of time so that one may pray later if that person is preoccupied. The prayers must be performed within these timeframes:

- Fajr [dawn] prayer: It consists of two units. It begins from the appearance of dawn[47] and lasts until the beginning of sunrise.[48]

- Ẓuhr [midday] prayer: It consists of four units. It begins after noon[49] when the sun begins to decline. This is determined when an object's shadow stops decreasing and

---

47 Dawn is when a line of light first appears and begins to spread across the horizon signaling the start of the day.

48 The beginning of sunrise is when the disc of the sun first appears above the horizon.

49 This refers to high noon when the sun crosses its highest point, not when it is 12:00pm.

begins to increase. It lasts until the shadow of an object [minus its shadow at noon[50]] equals the object itself.[51]

- ʿAsr [late-afternoon] prayer: It consists of four units. It begins when ẓuhr ends and lasts until the sun sets.

- Maghrib [evening] prayer: It consists of three units. It begins when ʿasr ends and lasts until the whiteness[52] after the reddish glow in the sky disappears and darkness spreads.

- ʿIshā' [night] prayer: It consists of 4 units. It begins when maghrib ends and lasts until the beginning of fajr.

There are many programs which calculate the exact times of prayer based on one's location. It is recommended to use these calculations and programs. However, there are some differences in the way they are calculated, especially the fajr and ʿishā' timings, so be aware of that. It is best to follow the timings of your local Muslim community.

It is recommended to not delay prayers without a reason. However, some prayers are better delayed when the community might benefit. Here are some general rules:

- If fajr is being prayed in a group it is recommended to delay it so that more people attend it in the mosque.

---

50 The curvature of the earth often results in a shadow even when the sun is directly overhead.

51 This is according to the Mālikī, Shāfiʿī, and Ḥanbalī schools as well as the two most distinguished students of Imām Abū Ḥanīfah: Abū Yūsuf and Muḥammad.

52 This is the opinion of Abū Ḥanīfah, although most of his followers differed from him.

- In very warm climates it is recommended to delay the ẓuhr prayer in summer so that it's easier for people to attend.

- The ʿasr prayer should not be delayed near the end of its time.

- The maghrib prayer should always be prayed at the beginning of its time.

- The ʿishāʾ prayer should not be delayed past midnight and you should not go to sleep before praying it, in case you don't wake up in time.

PREREQUISITES BEFORE PRAYER

Before praying, the following prerequisites must be met, otherwise the prayer will not count:

- Be in a state of purity by performing wuḍū or its substitute.

- Make sure your clothes, body, and place of prayer [where your body will touch] are free of impurities.

- Make sure your body is covered properly, even if you are alone. A male must cover what is between the navel and knees[53] while a woman must cover her entire body except the face, hands, and feet. If a small area is uncovered during prayer, it should be covered when detected. However, if a large area is uncovered, the prayer must be repeated.

---

53 Whether or not the knees and navel must be covered is a matter of dispute between Muslim scholars. If it is easy to do so it is always better to cover them.

- Face the qiblah [direction of the ka'bah in Makkah] with your chest. You may use a compass or calculate based on the position of the sun, moon, or stars. If you can't figure out the direction, estimate by looking at the direction of roads or by asking someone. If you discover that you were wrong after the prayer there is no need to repeat it since you tried your best. However, if you discover you are wrong during the prayer, turn towards the right direction. If unable to face the qiblah due to danger, illness, lack of space [i.e. on a plane], or any other reason you may pray in any direction.

- Make sure that the time for the prayer you are about to perform has entered.

HOW TO PRAY

Prayer consists of a number of units, or cycles, in which you repeat much of what you do and say in each unit. There are three different types of prayer: a two-unit, three-unit, and four-unit prayer. The five daily prayers consist of all three types.

The following is how a two-unit prayer is performed:

- Select a place to pray where you will not be disturbed. It is recommended to mark your place with either a large object in front of you [such as a chair] or by drawing a line so that no one crosses in front of your prayer area. If you are praying on a carpet, the edge of the carpet or the line drawn on it acts as a barrier for you.

- Intention [niyyah]: Make the intention immediately before starting that you plan to pray and be conscious of which prayer you are performing. This is done by focusing your thoughts.

- Standing [qiyām]: Stand up straight with your hands to your sides. Your feet should be pointing forward. Your feet should be spread apart the length of at least one hand span but no more than shoulder width apart.[54] Your eyes should be focused on the ground where you will prostrate. During the prayer you may close your eyes for concentration whenever you wish. This is the stance of a person at full attention who is focused.

- Raising Hands [rafʿ al-yadayn]: Begin the prayer by raising your hands near your ears. Make sure your palms are facing forward. This signifies that you are leaving all other thoughts in your mind behind as you begin connecting with Allah. It also signifies that you are surrendering yourself before the Lord of the Worlds and leaving your own desires for what he has commanded. While raising your hands [or right before or after] say the takbīr [glorification]:

اللّٰهُ أَكْبَرُ

allāhu akbar

Allah is the greatest

- Standing for Recitation [qirā'ah]: Lower your hands and use your right hand to grab your left one at the wrist or

54 Standing more than shoulder width apart would cause a gap between you and the people standing beside you [when praying in a group]. It is also considered undignified and therefore disliked.

forearm. Place both hands on your body either above or below your navel, or on the chest. This is a stance of humility which shows your awe and respect in front of Allah. After placing your hands, say the following:

- Opening Supplication [istiftāḥ]:

سُبْحَانَكَ اللَّهُمَّ وَبِحَمْدِكَ وَتَبَارَكَ اسْمُكَ وَتَعَالَى جَدُّكَ وَلَا إِلَهَ غَيْرُكَ

subḥānakallahumma wa biḥadmik wa tabārakasmuka
wa taʿālā jadduka wa lā ilāha ghayruk

Glory to you, Allah. May You be praised. Your name is blessed,
your greatness is exalted [over all others],
and no one is deserving of worship but You.

- Seeking Refuge [taʿawwudh]:

أَعُوذُ بِاللَّهِ مِنَ الشَّيْطَانِ الرَّجِيمِ

aʿūdhu billahi minash shayṭānir rajīm

I seek refuge in Allah from the cursed Satan

- Allah's Name [basmalah]:

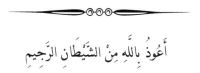

بِسْمِ اللّٰهِ الرَّحْمٰنِ الرَّحِيمِ

bismillahir raḥmānir raḥīm

In the name of Allah, the Compassionate, the Merciful

- Al-Fātiḥah: Recite sūrah al-Fātiḥah [first chapter of the Qur'an]. It is always recommended to recite the Qur'an in a melodic voice.

- Āmīn:

آمين

Āmīn

Accept this prayer

- Qur'an Recitation [qirā'ah]: Recite some Qur'an. It may consist of either a complete sūrah or a few verses. There is nothing specific which must be read in a particular prayer.

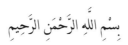

Bowing [rukūʿ]: Bend down and grab your knees while saying the takbīr. Keep your fingers slightly spread apart for support and to make grabbing your knees easier. Your eyes should be focused where your feet are. Try to keep your back straight as much as possible. This is a stance of humbling the body before Allah by lowering it in a bowing position. It should remind you of your place in front of Allah. Then say three times:

سُبْحَانَ رَبِّيَ الْعَظِيمِ

subḥāna rabbiyal aẓīm

Glory be to my Lord, the Great

- Intermediate Standing [qiyām]: Return to standing position while saying:

سَمِعَ اللّٰهُ لِمَنْ حَمِدَهُ رَبَّنَا لَكَ الْحَمْدُ

samiʿallāhu liman ḥamidah. Rabbanā lakal ḥamd.

Allah has heard the one who praised Him. Our Lord, you are praised.

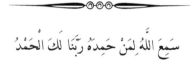

- Prostration [sajdah/sujūd]: Go into prostration by getting down on the floor while saying the takbīr. Put your forehead and nose on the ground between your hands. Keep your hands flat on the ground near your ears with your fingers together and facing forward. Make sure your elbows are off the ground and away from your sides. Also, keep space between your stomach and thighs so that your body is spread out. The bottom of your toes should be on the floor facing forward with the rest of your feet off the ground. This is a stance of the utmost humility where you put your face, which represents your honor, on the floor in front of Allah. Then say three times:

سُبْحَانَ رَبِّيَ الْأَعْلَى

subḥāna rabbiyal aʿlā

Glory be to my Lord, the Highest

- Intermediate Sitting [qaʿdah]: Rise up and sit on the floor while saying the takbīr. Sit with your palms on your thighs near the knees. Keep your fingers together. Your eyes should be directed at your knees. If you are able to, sit on your left foot while standing on the toes of your right foot which is a little out to the side. If this position is difficult, sit in any comfortable way. This is supposed to be a comfortable and relaxing position which gives you a break before prostrating again.

- Second Prostration [sajdah/sujūd]: Go into prostration again and say what you said before.

- Standing for Recitation [qiyām]: Say the takbīr and return to standing position with hands folded as before. This completes one unit of prayer.

- For the second unit, skip the Opening Supplication [istiftāḥ] and Seeking Refuge [taʿawwudh] but perform all the other steps as you did for the first unit up to the second prostration.

- Sitting [qaʿdah]: After prostrating, rise up and sit on the floor while saying the takbīr. Then say:

  - Salutations [taḥīyyāt]:

التَّحِيَّاتُ لِلَّهِ وَالصَّلَوَاتُ وَالطَّيِّبَاتُ السَّلَامُ عَلَيْكَ أَيُّهَا النَّبِيُّ وَرَحْمَةُ اللَّهِ وَبَرَكَاتُهُ
السَّلَامُ عَلَيْنَا وَعَلَى عِبَادِ اللهِ الصَّالِحِينَ

at-taḥiyyātu lillāhi wasṣ-ṣalawātu watṭ-ṭayyibātu
as-salāmu ʿalayka ayyuhan nabiyyu wa raḥmatullahi wa barakātuhu
as-salāmu ʿalaynā wa ʿalāʿibādillahiṣ ṣāliḥīn

Greetings, prayers, and all pure things ultimately belong to Allah.
May the peace of Allah be with you, Prophet,
as well as Allah's mercy and blessings. May the peace of Allah be
with us and with all of Allah's righteous servants.

  - Declaration of Faith [tashahhud] while making a fist with your right hand and pointing forward with your index finger:

أَشْهَدُ أَنْ لَا إِلَهَ إِلَّا اللَّهُ وَأَشْهَدُ أَنَّ مُحَمَّدًا عَبْدُهُ وَرَسُولُهُ

ash hadu allā ilāha illallah wa
ash hadu anna muḥammadan ʿabduhu wa rasūluhu

I declare that no one is deserving of worship besides Allah and that
Muhammad is His servant and messenger.

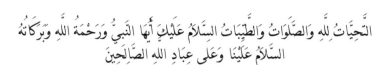

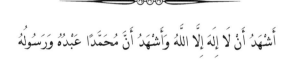

- Blessings [ṣalawāt]:

اللَّهُمَّ صَلِّ عَلَى مُحَمَّدٍ وَعَلَى آلِ مُحَمَّدٍ كَمَا صَلَّيْتَ عَلَى إِبْرَاهِيمَ وَعَلَى آلِ إِبْرَاهِيمَ
إِنَّكَ حَمِيدٌ مَجِيدٌ اللَّهُمَّ بَارِكْ عَلَى مُحَمَّدٍ وَعَلَى آلِ مُحَمَّدٍ كَمَا بَارَكْتَ عَلَى إِبْرَاهِيمَ
وَعَلَى آلِ إِبْرَاهِيمَ إِنَّكَ حَمِيدٌ مَجِيدٌ

allāhumma ṣalli ʿalā muḥammadin waʿalā āli muḥammadin kamā ṣallayta ʿalā ibrāhīma wa ʿalā āli ibrāhīma innaka ḥamīdum majīd. allāhumma bārik ʿalā muḥammadin wa ʿalā āli muḥammadin kamā bārakta ʿalā ibrāhīma wa ʿalā āli ibrāhīma innaka ḥamīdum majīd

Allah, bless Muhammad and his family, just as you have blessed Ibrāhīm and his family. You are the praiseworthy and glorious. Allah, favor Muhammad and his family, just as you have favored Ibrāhīm and his family. You are the praiseworthy and glorious.

- Supplication: You may make any supplications before concluding the prayer. It is preferable to memorize some that the Prophet used to make in the prayer.

- Greetings [taslīm]: Conclude the prayer by moving your head to the right and say the taslīm. Then move it to the left and say the same. You are praying for all the people around you and the angels to your sides. This is the taslīm:

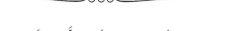

السَّلَامُ عَلَيْكُمْ وَرَحْمَةُ اللَّهِ

as-salāmu ʿalaykum wa raḥmatullah

May peace and mercy be on you.

When praying alone, it is recommended to whisper everything loud enough that you can at least hear yourself. Otherwise it is allowed to say the prayer in your mind as well.

A three unit prayer adds an extra unit after the Declaration of Faith [tashahhud] by saying the takbīr and returning to standing position with hands folded. This begins the third unit of prayer which is identical to the second one except that no Qur'an is recited after saying 'āmīn'. Sit after the second prostration and conclude the prayer as you would in the final sitting of a two-unit prayer.

A four unit prayer adds an extra unit after the second prostration of the third unit [there is no sitting after the second prostration]. Say the takbīr and return to standing position with hands folded. This begins the fourth unit of prayer which is identical to the second unit except that no Qur'an is recited after saying 'āmīn'. Then sit after the second prostration and conclude the prayer as you would in the final sitting of a two-unit prayer.

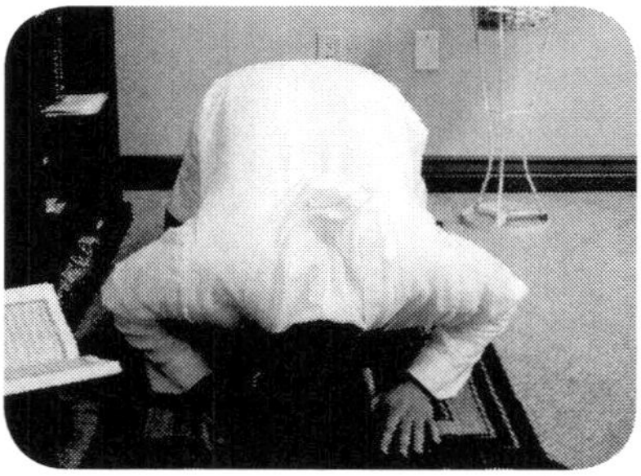

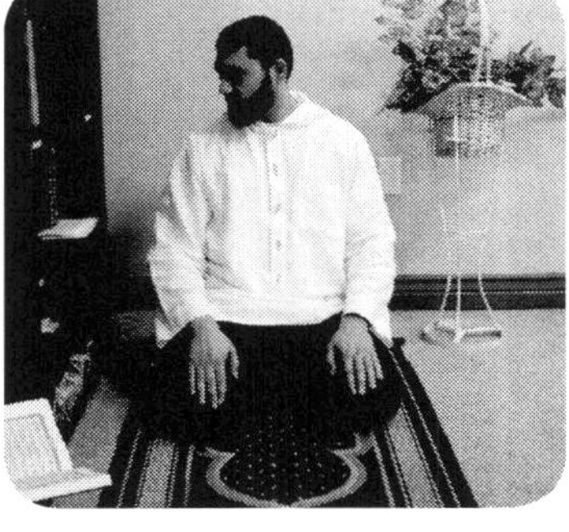

AFTER PRAYER

After the prayer is finished, it is recommended to remember Allah and supplicate to Him. These are only some of the recommended ways:

- To say:

اللَّهُمَّ أَعِنِّي عَلَى ذِكْرِكَ، وَشُكْرِكَ، وَحُسْنِ عِبَادَتِكَ

allāhummaa ʿinnīʿ alā dhikrika wa shukrika wa ḥusni ʿibādatik

Allah, help me to remember You, thank You,
and worship You in the best way.

- To say:

اللهُمَّ أَنْتَ السَّلَامُ وَمِنْكَ السَّلَامُ، تَبَارَكْتَ يَا ذَا الْجَلَالِ وَالْإِكْرَامِ

allāhumm aanta ssalām wa minka ssalām
tabārakta yā dhal jalāli wal ikrām

Allah, you are the source of peace and the provider of peace. You are the possessor of greatness and generosity.

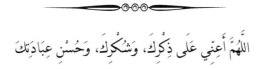

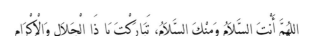

- To glorify Allah thirty three times, then to praise Him thirty three times, and then to extol Him thirty three times. It may also be done ten times each instead. The wordings are as follows:

سُبْحَانَ اللَّهِ | الْحَمْدُ لِلَّهِ | اللَّهُ أَكْبَرُ

subḥānallāh | alḥamdulillāh | allāhu akbar

Allah is glorified | Allah is praised | Allah is the greatest

INVALIDATING PRAYER

There are certain acts which cause your prayer to be nullified because they represent disrespect and disregard to the spiritual state of prayer:

⊛ Nullifying any of the prerequisites of prayer such as losing your wuḍū' or turning your chest away from the qiblah [direction of prayer]. Turning your head during prayer does not invalidate it but should only be done out of necessity.

⊛ Saying something that is not part of the prayer. If you need to signal someone during the prayer you may raise your voice and say "subḥānallah" ["Glory to Allah"] since praising Allah is part of the prayer. You may also briefly signal with your hand. Crying and moaning is recommended when praying alone and does not constitute speaking.

⊛ Performing several consecutive movements which are unnecessary and not part of the prayer. Some movements such as itching, covering your mouth when yawning, muting your phone, blowing your nose, or taking a few steps are all fine. You may carry children while praying but not speak to them.

- Laughing loud enough that your neighbor can hear it. If it is so quiet that only you can hear it, your prayer is not broken, but it is contrary to the purpose of prayer.

If there is a need to break your prayer, you may just leave. It is recommended to break your prayer in cases where someone is in danger, your possessions are being stolen, something is burning, or when you really need to relieve yourself.

DISLIKED ACTIONS IN PRAYER

The following actions are disliked during prayer but they do not invalidate it:

- Doing anything that may distract you from concentrating such as looking around, playing with your hands, unnecessarily moving around, etc.
- Praying when you are in a hurry such as when you need to relieve yourself, are very hungry and food is nearby, or are very tired.
- Wearing improper clothes which you would not wear in front of other people, since Allah is more deserving of your respect.
- Being in a place which distracts you such as praying on a carpet with several designs.

- Praying in a dirty or dangerous place such as near a dumpster, in a bathroom, or on a public road.

Group Prayer

PRAYING IN A GROUP has been urged upon Muslims in order to strengthen the bonds between them. It arouses in Muslims a spirit of unity and cooperation. The synchronous, military-like, precision of the group prayer also teaches a Muslim to be disciplined, organized, and to follow qualified leadership.

Muslims are encouraged to build and pray in mosques. Not only does it serve as a gathering place for Muslims to pray together in a group but also acts as a symbol that Islam is present in that society.

WHO SHOULD PRAY IN A GROUP

All adult males are strongly encouraged to pray every one of the five prayers in the mosque, or at least in a group with other Muslims. If one intends to pray in a group but is unable due to an excuse, he receives the same reward as if he did pray in a group. The following are valid excuses for missing a group prayer:

- A person is ill.

- The weather is extreme which might cause an illness.

- There is heavy rain, mud, or traffic which makes it difficult to reach the mosque.
- There is a danger to one's family or property.
- There are no other Muslims nearby that are willing to pray in a group.

Women and children should not be discouraged from attending the mosque unless there is a reason that makes it preferable for them to stay at home such as living in a dangerous environment.

ADHĀN [CALL TO PRAYER] AND IQĀMAH [CALL TO INITIATE]

Calling people to prayer has been instituted in order to remind and alert Muslims that it is time to pray. Instead of using a horn or bell, as Jews and Christians do, the human voice is used. The adhān is the call to notify people that the time for prayer has entered and the iqāmah is a signal that the prayer is about to start. Both of them are recommended for the five daily prayers[55], whether praying alone or in a group.

Adhān

The adhān must be called after the time for prayer has entered.[56] The person calling should stand and face the direction of prayer. It is also recommended for the caller to place their index fingers in the ears and be in a state of wuḍū'.

55 It is also recommended for the Friday prayer, but not for any other prayer.

56 However, the adhān for fajr may be called before the time to wake people up.

Then the caller should say the following words loudly and in a melodic voice:

اللهُ أَكْبَرُ اللهُ أَكْبَرُ

allāhu akbar. allāhu akbar.

Allah is the greatest. Allah is the greatest.

اللهُ أَكْبَرُ اللهُ أَكْبَرُ

allāhu akbar. allāhu akbar.

Allah is the greatest. Allah is the greatest.

أَشْهَدُ أَنْ لَا إِلٰهَ إِلَّا اللهُ

ash-hadu allā ilāha illallah.

I declare that there is no god besides Allah.

أَشْهَدُ أَنْ لَا إِلٰهَ إِلَّا اللهُ

ash-hadu allā ilāha illallah.

I declare that there is no god besides Allah.

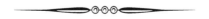

أَشْهَدُ أَنَّ مُحَمَّدًا رَسُولُ اللهِ

ash-hadu anna muḥammadar rasūlullah.

I declare that Muhammad is the Messenger of Allah.

أَشْهَدُ أَنَّ مُحَمَّدًا رَسُولُ اللهِ

ash-hadu anna muḥammadar rasūlullah.

I declare that Muhammad is the messenger of Allah.

حَيَّ عَلَى الصَّلَاة

ḥayya ʿala ṣṣalāh.

Come to prayer.

حَيَّ عَلَى الصَّلَاةِ

ḥayya ʿala ṣṣalāh.

Come to prayer.

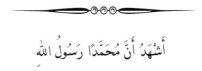

حَيَّ عَلَى الْفَلَاحِ

ḥayya ʿalal falāḥ.

Come to success.

حَيَّ عَلَى الْفَلَاحِ

ḥayya ʿalal falāḥ.

Come to success.

اللّٰهُ أَكْبَرُ اللّٰهُ أَكْبَرُ

allāhu akbar. allāhu akbar.

Allah is the greatest. Allah is the greatest.

لَا إِلَٰهَ إِلَّا اللّٰهُ

lā ilāha illallāh.

There is no god besides Allah.

It is recommended when saying "ḥayya ʿala ṣṣalāh" to turn the head to the right both times and when saying "ḥayya ʿalal falāḥ" to turn the head to the left both times. It is also recommended to pause shortly between every statement as presented.

When calling for the fajr prayer, it is recommended to add the following after "ḥayya ʿalal falāḥ":

الصَّلاةُ خَيْرٌ مِنَ النَّوْمِ

aṣ-ṣalātu khayrum minan nawm.

Prayer is better than sleep.

الصَّلاةُ خَيْرٌ مِنَ النَّوْمِ

aṣ-ṣalātu khayrum minan nawm.

Prayer is better than sleep.

Iqāmah

The iqāmah is called right before the group prayer is about to begin. The iqāmah should only be performed when the imam is ready. The wording of the iqāmah is the same as the adhān except that after saying "come to prayer" you add the following:

قَدْ قَامَتِ الصَّلَاةُ قَدْ قَامَتِ الصَّلَاةُ

qad qāmati ṣṣalātu. qad qāmati ṣṣalāh.

The prayer has stood up. The prayer has stood up.

It is better not to pause between statements and to say the iqāmah quickly.

Responding to the Adhān

The people who hear the adhān are recommended to remain quiet and respond by repeating each phrase after it is said except "come to prayer" and "come to success", in which they say:

لَا حَوْلَ وَلَا قُوَّةَ إِلَّا بِاللهِ

lā ḥawla walā quwwata illā billāh

No one really has power or might besides Allah

Also, after hearing "prayer is better than sleep" say:

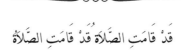

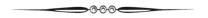

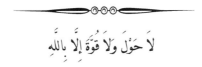

صَدَقْتَ وَبَرَرْتَ

ṣadaqta wa bararta

You have spoken the truth and been honest

After the adhān is complete, both the caller and the listener should make a special prayer for the Prophet as follows:

اللَّهُمَّ رَبَّ هَذِهِ الدَّعْوَةِ التَّامَّةِ، وَالصَّلَاةِ الْقَائِمَةِ آتِ مُحَمَّدًا الْوَسِيلَةَ وَالْفَضِيلَةَ وَابْعَثْهُ مَقَامًا مَحْمُودًا الَّذِي وَعَدْتَهُ

allāhumma rabba hādhihid daʿwati ttāmmah waṣṣalātil qā'imah āti muḥammadan al-wasīlata wal faḍīlatal wabʿathhu maqāman maḥmūdan allladhī waʿadtah.

Allah, Lord of this comprehensive invitation and enduring prayer, grant Muhammad a place near you and an exalted station. Bestow on him the praiseworthy status that you have promised him.

IMĀM [PRAYER LEADER] AND FOLLOWERS

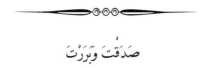

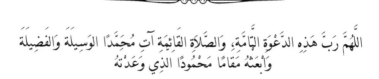

One person is chosen to lead the group and is known as the imām of the prayer. The rest of the people following form lines behind him standing side by side with their shoulders touching. This serves as a lesson in humility and equality where no one has any privileged position regardless of their wealth, race, or social status.

If there are women or children present, they will form their own lines with the lines of children coming after the men and the lines of women coming after the children. This is done for reasons of modesty and to keep an eye on the children. It is not a problem if children stand in the line with either the men or women.

If there are only two people praying together, the follower stands to the right of the imām, with both of them forming one line. However, if only one male and one female are praying together, she will stand behind him in a separate row. If only women decide to pray in a group, the female imām will stand in the middle of the row and lead.

No line should consist of only one person. A person who comes late and finds the line full should gesture one of the people in that row to move back so there will be two people in the line. The people in that row should move and fill the gap in. However, if there is only one woman present, she must be alone in her own line and not join the men.

There should be no unnecessary barriers or gaps between the rows. An example of a necessary gap would be a public walkway or a street where people should not pray. The follower must be performing the same prayer as the imām. However, if he has already prayed that prayer, he may pray it again with the imām and it will count as an extra prayer.

HOW TO LEAD

The imām should remind the people to straighten their lines and ensure that they are even before commencing the prayer.

The imām will then begin and say the following parts of the prayer out loud:

- Every *takbīr.*
- The statement "samiʿallahu liman ḥamidah".
- Both greetings [*taslīms*].

During the fajr, maghrib, and 'ishā' prayers, the imām will also recite all verses from the Qur'an out loud while standing in the first two units of each prayer.[57] This is probably because most people don't work during these hours and the group is larger. The people behind him will listen attentively to the verses being recited. The rest of the prayer will be silent, so one should whisper loud enough to hear oneself. Everyone must follow the leader in the movements of the prayer.

When the imām says something out loud, it counts for the follower and does not need to be repeated, otherwise, the follower is to say the prescribed parts of the prayer whenever the imām is silent.[58]

The follower must not precede the imām or lag behind him. If one precedes or lags behind more than one movement in the prayer, the prayer is invalid. If the imām moves to the next part of the prayer before the follower has finished, they must also do so because following the imām takes precedence. If the imām makes a mistake in prayer and performs two additional prostrations for having made a mistake[59], the follower must also do so, even if they didn't make

57 Saying "bismillahir raḥmānir raḥīm" should be silent. Also "āmīn" may be silent or said aloud by all the followers.

58 This is the opinion of Mālik.

59 There is a separate section on Mistakes in Prayer in the following pages.

that mistake. However, if the follower makes a mistake but the imām does not, no extra prostrations are required. Furthermore, if the imām is injured and must sit, the followers remain standing since they do not have the same injury. If the imām forgets to sit in the final sitting and adds another unit of prayer, the follower should not join him and wait until he sits back down.

The imām should lengthen the recitation of the first unit a little more than the second so that people who are late can catch the entire prayer. He should not prolong recitation or any other actions of the prayer which might make it difficult on people who must work or have back problems. If a child is crying or there is some other event which may distract someone, the recitation should be shortened.

If the prayer of the imām is incorrect according to his own opinion [e.g. he does not have wuḍū' because he only wiped part of his head but he believes the entire head must be wiped] then the prayer of the follower is also incomplete and must be repeated. If the imām needs to leave or loses his wuḍū' he should turn around, find the most qualified person behind him to lead and appoint him to be the imām. That person should continue as the imām from where he left off. If he is standing, he should move forward to the position of imām, otherwise he can lead from where he is. When the first imām returns, he may rejoin the group as a follower.

If a follower loses his wuḍū', he must stop praying and leave. If there are too many rows and no nearby exits, he should stop his prayer and sit down until the prayer is over. There is no need to be embarrassed and a person may close his eyes and bow his head to avoid unnecessary attention.

When the prayer is finished the imām should move a little from his place so that anyone coming late knows the prayer is over.

MOST DESERVING TO LEAD PRAYER

The person most deserving to lead the prayer is, in order of priority:

- The official leader of the Muslims, if there is one.
- The one who is most knowledgeable about the rules of prayer.
- The one who is the most knowledgeable in how to recite the Qur'an.
- The one who has the most Qur'an memorized.
- The one who is known to be the most pious.

A person employed by a mosque to lead has first preference in that mosque. Also, a man in his own house has preference over others. However, any of the people who are more qualified can allow another person to lead the prayer, if they choose to.

CORRECTING A MISTAKE

If the imām makes a mistake in prayer, one of the followers should raise his voice and say سُبْحَانَ اللهِ [subḥānallah; Allah is glorious] in order to remind him. A woman should clap her right hand over the back of her left hand loud enough for the imām to hear. When the imām realizes his mistake, he should fix it and perform two additional prostrations.

If the imām makes a mistake while reciting the Qur'ān, one of the followers may correct him by reciting that part of the verse out loud. The imām should understand that he is being corrected and repeat the part where he made the mistake. If the imām pauses during recitation and it is clear that he cannot remember what comes next, one of the followers may remind him by reciting part of the verse out loud.

JOINING LATE

If you are late to the prayer, do not rush but walk normally. If you join the group after the prayer has already begun, raise your hands, say the takbīr, and join the imām at whichever position he is. If you join the imām before he raises his head from bowing, you have caught that unit of the prayer, otherwise you missed it. When the prayer is about to end, let the imām conclude the prayer with the greetings [taslīm], but do not follow him in that. Remain seated until he finishes, then say the takbīr and stand back up to complete the missed units of the prayer. There are three things which must be determined when completing the prayer:

- The amount of units to make up: Calculate how many times you bowed with the imām and subtract that number from how many units the prayer was.

- When to recite verses of the Qur'an after al-Fātiḥah: You should always recite additional verses in the first two make-up units only. If you missed only one or two units of prayer, recite some verses in all make-up units. If you missed three or four units of prayer, recite in the first two but not in the third or fourth.

- When to perform the first sitting [*qaʿdah*] in a three or four unit prayer: You should perform the first sitting after having performed an even number of units. This should include the units you prayed with the imām. Add the total units you prayed alone and with the imām to determine when to perform the first sitting of prayer.

For example, if you catch one unit of the maghrib prayer with the imām you will recite Qur'an after al-fātiḥah in the first make up unit and will sit after it. Then you will stand up, recite only al-fātiḥah, and complete the prayer. If you caught two units of the ẓuhr prayer you will recite Qur'an after al-Fātiḥah in the first make up unit and will stand up and do the same for the second make up unit. Then you will complete the prayer.

Concentration and Humility in Prayer

A PRAYER DEVOID of spirit and concentration, even if performed perfectly in the physical sense, is like a fruit which may appear clean and pure on the outside but is actually rotten and spoiled on the inside. The Prophet once saw a man praying hastily and kept on telling him to repeat his prayer until he learned to slow down and have serenity in his movements.

Whenever you pray, try to act upon the following tips to help you increase concentration and spiritual presence during prayer:

- Before beginning the prayer, clear your mind from all other thoughts. Make sure to mute anything that might distract you during prayer.

- If you notice that your surroundings are distracting you, close your eyes. It is better to pray in a place where there are no distractions.

- Say every part of the prayer by moving your lips and whispering loud enough that you can hear yourself. This will help you to slow down as well as stay focused.

- Understand the meaning of what you are saying during prayer by reading at least the translation of the Arabic phrases. Reflect on the meaning while saying every phrase or with a brief pause whenever necessary.

- Whenever you say the *takbīr* during every transition to another position, realize that you are saying "Allah is the greatest". This means that He is greater than whatever thought might have been distracting you right before you made this statement. The transition to another position is where many people lose their focus. However, through this reflection, it can be a means to regain focus instead.

Mistakes in Prayer

MAJOR MISTAKES

IF ANY of the following parts of the prayer are not performed properly the prayer will not count and must be repeated because these are among the fundamental parts of praying:

- Intention.

- Beginning the prayer with the *takbīr.*

- Standing for Recitation. If unable due to an illness or being in a tight airplane then it is overlooked.

- Reciting some Qur'an.

- Bowing.

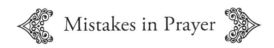

- Intermediate Standing.
- Prostrating twice.
- Sitting in the final unit of prayer long enough to reach the Declaration of Faith [*tashahhud*].
- Moving the head to the right and saying at least one greeting [*taslīm*].

If any of these essential acts are skipped during prayer you should return back to that action when you remember. If you complete the prayer without fulfilling all of these, prayer is not valid and must be repeated when you realize the mistake.

MINOR MISTAKES

If one makes a mistake in prayer which is not one of the requirements, the prayer is still valid but should be corrected by making two extra prostrations at the end. This will make up for any deficiencies in the prayer and will humiliate your ego which distracted you from prayer.

The following are common mistakes which require a person to perform two extra prostrations at the end of the prayer:

- Delaying one of the required acts of prayer because they must be done in the prescribed order.
- Forgetting to recite other verses of the Qur'an after al-Fātiḥah.
- Forgetting the first sitting in a three or four unit prayer by standing up after prostration. If you have stood up, stay

standing and continue the prayer. If you remember while attempting to stand up, sit back down.

- Reciting aloud when you're supposed to be silent, or vice versa in a group prayer.
- Adding an extra act of prayer such as performing three prostrations or two bowings in one unit.
- Skipping one of the following essential acts of prayer:
  - Raising the hands at the beginning of prayer.
  - Reciting al-fātiḥah.
  - Reciting a *sūrah* after al-fātiḥah in the first and second unit of prayer.
  - Saying the takbīr when transitioning from one act to another.
  - Saying the prescribed words during the intermediate standing.
  - Saying the prescribed words during both bowing and prostration.
  - Saying the salutations [*taḥīyyāt*], declaration of faith [*tashahhud*], and blessings [*ṣalawāt*] in the final sitting.
- If you stand up after the final prostration, sit back down and make the extra prostrations.
- If you conclude the prayer and then realize that you missed one or more units, stand up immediately, perform the omitted units, and make two extra prostrations.

If you are unsure how many units you have prayed so far and this forgetfulness rarely happens to you, stop your prayer and start again. If this does happen to you at least once a year then go with what seems most probable. For example, if you are *quite sure* that you have prayed four units but think that you *might* have prayed only three, assume that you have prayed four. If you cannot decide and are fifty-fifty between the two options, go with the lesser number and make the extra two prostrations. [see Appendix 1 for details]

HOW TO PERFORM THE PROSTRATION OF FORGETFULNESS

It is necessary to perform two additional prostrations at the end of the prayer if it is for a correctible mistake. There are two ways to perform it:

- Method 1:
  - Near the end of the prayer, just before you move your head towards the right, say the *takbīr* and make two prostrations as you would normally do in prayer.
  - Upon rising up from the second prostration, complete the prayer by making the final two greetings [*taslīm*] to the right and left.
- Method 2:
  - Near the end of the prayer, say only one greeting [*taslīm*] while moving your head to the right.
  - Say the takbīr and make two prostrations.
  - Upon rising up from the second prostration, repeat everything that was said in the final sitting of the prayer and then conclude with the two greetings [*taslīm*].

If you made more than one mistake in the prayer you will still only make two prostrations. This is because the prostrations signify that a mistake occurred in the prayer, regardless of the number. If you forget to prostrate after making a mistake, you may do so after the prayer is over. However, if the time for the prayer is over, then there is no need to do so anymore.

Missing and Making Up Prayer

BEING LAZY in observing prayer on time reflects your attitude towards Allah. Try to never miss a single prayer. In case you do miss one, make it up with a feeling of regret as soon as you are able to do so. If you forgot or slept through a prayer, you will not be held accountable for missing the prayer. However, you must try to prevent it from happening in the future by setting an alarm or reminder.

If you realize later that your prayer was invalid due to some reason [such as not having performed wuḍū' properly], it must be made up. Remember that this only applies when you are certain and should not be based on doubts [see Appendix 1].

It is recommended to make adhān and iqāmah for a missed prayer. However, if you have missed more than one prayer, only one adhān is recommended for all the missed prayers. The prayers must be made up in order unless you have missed more than five prayers. In that case, it is recommended to pray in order and specify the missed prayers as much as possible.

One who was raised in a non-practicing Muslim family or society such that one was not taught how to pray properly or not told about the importance and necessity of prayer does not need to make up those missed prayers but instead ask Allah for forgiveness.

Friday [Jumu'ah] Prayer

THE IMPORTANCE of praying in a group has already been explained in detail. However, there will be times throughout the week where people are occupied and not able to make it to the mosque at the same time. Therefore, Friday prayer serves as a time where the entire local Muslim community will gather in a group together. This will let them meet each other, find out who is ill or in need, and pray together. Friday is considered the best day of the week for Muslims and is a distinguishing mark for them, the way that Jews observe Saturday and Christians observe Sunday as their religious days. It is also a time to be reminded about your duties as a Muslim and to be conscious of Allah by listening to the sermons.

WHO MUST ATTEND

All adult males must attend the Friday prayer. They are only excused if they are traveling, ill, or will encounter some severe difficulty were they to attend.[60] Women are not

60 A person may pray ẓuhr at home if it is very difficult to attend due to snow or heavy rain. Also, a student who has an exam that cannot be delayed or an employee who has an urgent meeting that would result

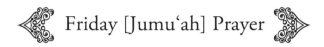

required to attend since they may be tending to the needs of children or the household. However, it is recommended that they try to attend as well since they are also in need of admonition and meeting others. Whoever does not attend must pray ẓuhr because Friday prayer is a substitute for that.

CONDITIONS

The timing of the Friday prayer is the same as the ẓuhr prayer and it must be prayed within this timeframe. In order to have a Friday prayer, there must be at least three people present, including the imām.[61] It may be prayed in any mosque, building, or even in an open area.

HOW IT IS CONDUCTED

An imām should be selected to deliver two sermons and lead the prayers. This is how it should be performed:

- The first adhān is called at least a few minutes before the sermon begins.
- The imām stands, faces the congregation, greets them, then sits down.
- A person performs the call to prayer near the imām.
- The imām stands up and delivers the first sermon. He should begin by praising Allah and praying for the Prophet in Arabic. The rest of the sermon may be in the local

---

in losing one's job if missed may be excused. However, a person must try everything in one's ability to be excused from such occurrences.

61 This is the opinion of Abū Yūsuf and Muḥammad.

language and should include admonition and reminding people to be devout Muslims.

- When the first sermon is complete, the imām sits down for about the same time that one sits between two prostrations.

- He then stands back up and delivers a second sermon which should begin by praising Allah and praying for the Prophet again. The second sermon may consist of more admonition followed by a general supplication.

- When the second sermon is done, the imām signals that the prayer should begin. A person calls the iqāmah and the imām leads the people in a two unit prayer. The Qur'an is recited out loud like in the fajr prayer due to the large amount of people. This suffices for the ẓuhr prayer, so whoever joined the imām before one completed the prayer does not need to pray ẓuhr.[62]

There is a lot of flexibility in how to deliver the two sermons. The only requirements are that each of them must contain words praising Allah and praying for the Prophet. The imām should not make the sermons too long since there may be people who have other appointments to attend to.

ETIQUETTE OF THE FRIDAY PRAYER

It is recommended to take a bath on Friday before attending the prayer. It is also recommended to avoid eating garlic, onions, or anything else that will emit a strong distasteful odor.[63]

---

62 This is the opinion of Abū Ḥanīfah and Abū Yūsuf.

63 Smoking cigarettes are prohibited in Islam due to the severe health effects. However, if a Muslim decides to smoke anyways, they should

Before arriving at the mosque, it is recommended to brush your teeth and wear perfume. Friday is also a good day to cut your nails and remove unwanted body hair.

No one is allowed to talk during the sermons so that everyone is able to concentrate. Even if you see someone else talking, you should gesture them to be quiet without saying anything. It is also not allowed for anyone to conduct business transactions during the sermons.

It is recommended to pray four units after the Friday prayer. Any number of units may be prayed before the sermon begins. However, once the imām has begun the sermon, it is disliked to begin a new prayer.

Prayer When Injured or Ill

IF YOU ARE injured and not able to stand, you may sit down while making sure to bow and prostrate fully. If unable to bow or prostrate, you do not even need to stand and may perform the bowing and prostration through gestures. You must bow down lower when gesturing for prostration than for the bowing. If unable to even sit, you may lie down and pray through gestures, either on your back with your feet facing the qiblah[64] or on your side with your face towards the qiblah.

---

never allow that odor to affect people in the mosque through third-hand smoke.

64 So that the face is turned toward Makkah.

Prayer remains an obligation as long as you are conscious. If you can barely move, you may pray through gestures with your eyes or pray in your heart. Also, if you find it painful to be moved in the direction of the qiblah, you may pray in the direction you are.

Whoever is unconscious for five prayers or less must make them up after waking. If one is out for longer than that, there is no need to make them up.

Prayer When Traveling

TRAVELING IS CONSIDERED to be a hardship for most people since it is physically exhausting and also disturbs the eating and sleeping patterns. In order to make things easy on a person undergoing such a journey, Allah has prescribed special concessions for such people. These include wiping over the socks for a longer period of time, shortening prayers, skipping the Friday prayer, and even being allowed to postpone a fast.

SHORTENING PRAYER

When you are classified as being a traveler, all four unit prayers are reduced to two units. This is to make it easier for you to complete your prayers while still making sure to worship Allah.

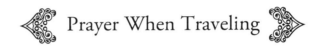

When you make the intention to travel you begin shortening your prayers as soon as you leave your city. This reduction lasts until you return to your city or enter an area with the intention of remaining there for a significant amount of time.[65] However, if you are unsure of how long you are staying and predict that you might leave any day, you may continue to shorten even if this uncertain situation lasts for months.

If a traveler prays behind an imām who is not traveling, they follow the imām and pray four units. However, if the imām is a traveler and a follower is not, the follower should stand up after the imām finishes and pray two more units. It is recommended for the imām to make an announcement that they are a traveler immediately before and after the prayer so that no one is confused.

If you miss a prayer while traveling, it is like a debt and you must make it up as two units even after you have returned home. The same applies if you miss a prayer before traveling and then want to make it up while traveling: you pray four.

MINIMUM DISTANCE

There is no specific definition of what is considered a journey so people will have to judge according to their mode of transportation and how much difficulty they will undergo.[66] A

65 This has been estimated to be between four and twenty days. The traveler will have to decide this duration based on the level of hardship involved. It is recommended to not set this limit greater than fifteen days since this is the opinion of the Hanafī school, which is the most liberal of the four schools on this issue.

66 This is the opinion of Ibn Taymiyyah. Scholars have tried to set limits to make things easier for people, but the means of transportation have drastically changed since the 20th century. There are many variables that must be taken into consideration when determining whether a person is traveling such as whether it is by plane, ship, or car. Traffic may also play a factor in determining the duration of travel. Therefore, it is recommended to not set specific restrictions

good way to determine whether you are 'traveling' is to make sure that at least most of the following apply:

- You have traveled at last fifty miles, one way.
- You would describe yourself as 'traveling'. For example, if you commute eighty miles to work, you are 'commuting' not 'traveling'.
- You have packed your bags and supplies for this journey.
- You let your neighbors know that you are traveling.
- You have left your city/county of residence and crossed to another city/county.

AIR TRAVEL

When traveling on an airplane [or even on a train], it is better to delay the prayer if it will reach its destination before the time of prayer is over. There are a few factors involved which may dictate concessions:

- Finding space to pray: If there is not enough space to perform prayer [or you are not allowed to stand in those areas] you should pray in your seat and gesture for bowing and prostration like an injured person would do.
- Determining the right direction: If you have sufficient space to bow and prostrate, you must try to determine the direction of prayer by asking a flight attendant who will ask the pilot. If there is no space, you may pray in any direction your seat is facing.

---

but leave it to the individual to determine [as sincerely as possible] whether they are traveling or not.

- Calculating the time for prayer: It is not very difficult to determine the fajr, maghrib, and ʿishāʾ prayers while flying over a region by looking out the window or asking the flight attendant to check for you.

COMBINING PRAYERS

It is always recommended to pray every prayer on time. However, if you face difficulty while traveling you may combine the ẓuhr and ʿasr prayers together by praying them in either of their times.[67] However, you must have the intention to combine before the time for ẓuhr elapses, or you will be held responsible for neglecting your prayer. The maghrib and ʿishāʾ prayers can also be combined in either of their times. There should not be a long gap between the two prayers when combining.

Extra Prayers

BESIDES THE five daily prayers there are others which are recommended for Muslims to pray whenever possible. Some of them are highly recommended, while others are merely encouraged if one has the time or feels the need to perform them.

WITR

One of the most emphasized prayers is the witr prayer. This can be prayed any time after praying ʿishāʾ but before the time for fajr enters. It is recommended to delay the witr prayer to

67 This is the opinion of the Shāfiʿī and Ḥambalī schools.

the last third of the night. However, if you aren't used to waking up early it is better to pray it before sleeping so that you do not miss it. There are several ways to pray the witr prayer. One way to perform it is very similar to a three unit maghrib prayer. After surah al-fātiḥah, it is recommended to recite surah al-aʿlā in the first unit, al-kāfirūn in the second, and al-ikhlās in the third. After reciting Qur'an in the third unit, say the *takbīr* and raise your hands to your ears as you would at the beginning of prayer. Lower them back as they were or let them hang at the sides and then recite the qunūt supplication as follows[68]:

اللَّهُمَّ اهْدِنِي فِيمَنْ هَدَيْتَ، وَعَافِنِي فِيمَنْ عَافَيْتَ، وَتَوَلَّنِي فِيمَنْ تَوَلَّيْتَ، وَبَارِكْ لِي فِيمَا أَعْطَيْتَ، وَقِنِي شَرَّ مَا قَضَيْتَ، إِنَّكَ تَقْضِي وَلَا يُقْضَى عَلَيْكَ، وَإِنَّهُ لَا يَذِلُّ مَنْ وَالَيْتَ، تَبَارَكْتَ رَبَّنَا وَتَعَالَيْتَ

allāhumma h-dinīfī man hadayt waʿāfinī fī man ʿāfayt wa tawallanī fī man tawallayt wa bārik lī fī mā aʿṭayt wa qinī sharra mā qaḍayt innaka taqḍī wa lā yuqḍāʿalayk wa innahu lā yadhillu mawwālayt tabārakta rabbanā wa taʿālayt

Allah, guide me like those you have guided, protect me like those you have protected, guard me like those you have guarded, bless me in what you have given me, and save me from the evil which you have decreed. You decree and nothing can be decreed against you. Whomever you support can never be disgraced. You are blessed, Lord, and high above all.

Then complete the third unit as normal. If you forget to perform the qunūt supplication, it is considered to be a

68 Whoever has not memorized this supplication yet may say "subḥānallah" three times.

correctible mistake and may be compensated with two additional prostrations at the end of the prayer. It is also recommended for a person who misses the witr prayer to make it up.

Witr is such an important prayer that it is recommended to make it up if missed. If making it up before sunrise, it may be prayed as normal. However, if it is made up after sunrise, it should be made up as a four unit prayer because an even number of units is preferred during the daytime.

PRAYERS CONNECTED WITH THE FIVE

Most people will fall short in performing their daily prayers. One way of compensating for these shortcomings is to perform additional prayers beyond the bare minimum prescribed ones. When performing the five daily prayers, it is recommended to pray the following prayers along with them:

- Two units before fajr. These should be brief by reciting short sūrahs. This is a highly recommended prayer and should not be missed. If fajr prayer is missed, it is recommended to make up these two units as well. If you join a group prayer and do not have time to perform this prayer, it may be prayed immediately after fajr.

- Two or four units before the ẓuhr prayer and two or four units after it.

- Two units after the maghrib prayer.

- Two units after the ʿishā' prayer.

These prayers not only merit reward and bring you closer to Allah but they also help to compensate for mistakes and inattention made in your five required prayers.

It is permissible to sit during these prayers even without an excuse, but the reward for the prayer will be half of what it would be if you stand. This is because sitting during prayer requires about half the effort of standing. When traveling, these prayers may even be performed while sitting in a car [but are not recommended while driving due to the danger involved] and the person would not need to face the direction of prayer [qiblah].

WHEN NOT TO PRAY

Additional prayers can be performed at any time since Allah is always deserving of praise and willing to listen to His servants. However, it is disliked to pray during the following times:

- After the fajr and ʿasr prayer has been performed. However, if there is a reason to pray such as making up a missed prayer or performing the funeral prayer, it is fine. It is also fine to read Qur'an or remember Allah.

- During sunrise and sunset which last about fifteen minutes each. These are the times when people who worship the sun pray, so Muslims should avoid it in order to be different. The only exception to the rule is that it is allowed to pray the ʿasr prayer during this time, although it should not have been delayed in the first place.

SUNRISE PRAYER

There is a prayer that is recommended between the fajr and ẓuhr prayer. It consists of two or four units. It can be performed about fifteen minutes after sunrise anytime before the start of ẓuhr.

NIGHT PRAYERS

Praying at night is better than extra prayers during the day because it is when most [normal] people sleep. The night prayers may be performed any time after the ʿishāʾ prayer but the best time to pray them is the last third of the night after sleeping. It is recommended to pray between two to eight units consisting of two-unit prayers each. If you have not already performed the witr prayer, it is recommended to conclude the night prayers with it.

PRAYER WHEN ENTERING THE MOSQUE

When entering a mosque it is recommended to pray at least two units before sitting down. If a person has already sat down they may still perform this prayer. If the person begins another prayer such as the prayer for that time, it will count as having fulfilled the prayer for entering the mosque. That is because the wisdom behind it is to honor the mosque by praying in it. Only one of these prayers with that intention is recommended per day in one mosque.

Funeral Prayer

DEATH IS a fact of life that no one denies. The funeral prayer has been sanctioned to honor a dead Muslim and to pray for them.

WHO MUST PRAY

The funeral prayer is a collective obligation on the Muslim community. As long as some Muslims prepare the deceased Muslim for burial and pray over them, the responsibility will be fulfilled. However, if no one does so, every Muslim living in that community will be held responsible for neglecting this duty.

CONDITIONS

The deceased must be a Muslim. The dead body must be present and prepared for burial. In case someone has been buried without being prayed over, you may pray in front of the grave if the burial was recent.

HOW TO PRAY

The prayer only consists of standing, with no bowing, prostration, or sitting. The deceased is placed in front of the imām while the followers line up as normal behind him.

- The prayer begins as usual with the imām saying the takbīr and raising his hands, then folding the right over the left.
- Then al-fātiḥah is to be recited silently by everyone.
- The imām says another takbīr while raising his hands and them folding them.
- Then everyone silently recites the blessings [ṣalawāt].
- The imām says another takbīr while raising his hands and them folding them.

- Then everyone silently supplicates for the deceased. One of the supplications may be:

اللَّهُمَّ اغْفِرْ لِحَيِّنَا وَمَيِّتِنَا وَشَاهِدِنَا وَغَائِبِنَا وَصَغِيرِنَا وَكَبِيرِنَا وَذَكَرِنَا وَأُنْثَانَا

allāhumma gh-fir li ḥayyinā wa mayyitinā wa shāhidinā wa ghā'ibinā wa ṣaghīrinā wa kabīrinā wa dhakarinā wa unthānā

Allah, forgive our living and dead, our present and absent, our young and old, and our male and female.

- The imām says another takbīr while raising his hands and them folding them.

- The imām concludes the prayer as normal by saying the greetings [taslīm]while standing and the people do the same.

Prostration of Recitation

IT IS RECOMMENDED [69] to prostrate after reciting or hearing certain Qur'anic verses which emphasize humility before Allah. There are fourteen places in the Qur'an and they are as follows: 7:206, 13:15, 16:50, 17:109, 19:58, 22:18, 25:60, 27:26, 32:15, 38:24, 41:38, 53:62, 84:21, and 96:19.

69 This is according to the Shāfiʿī school.

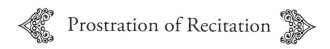

If you recite one of these verses during prayer, and intend on reciting more verses, you should say the *takbīr* and go into prostration immediately. Perform the prostration as normal, say the *takbīr*, return to standing position, and continue reciting from the next verse. The followers behind an imām should do the same. However, if a follower recites a verse of prostration while praying behind an imām, he does not prostrate since he is to follow the imām.

If you decide to stop at a prostration verse and not continue reciting more because it is the last verse in the sūrah [or for some other reason], you will continue the prayer as normal by going into bowing. This is because you will be going to prostrate in a few moments anyways.

If you are not engaged in prayer and recite one of these verses, you should stand, say the *takbīr* [without raising hands], and go into prostration. Perform prostration as in prayer, say the *takbīr*, and sit up. The prostration is complete. Remember that you must be in a state of purity, be properly covered, and face the qiblah [direction of prayer].

If outside of prayer you are reciting the Qur'an or hear someone else reciting one of these verses, you should prostrate at your leisure. It can be done immediately or may be delayed a little while. If you hear a recording of a person reciting, it is still recommended to prostrate because the effect on the listener may be the same as if it were live.

If you continue to repeat one verse of prostration because you are trying to memorize it or enjoy reciting it, only one prostration is recommended to be made.

Appendix 1:

Doubt Does Not Remove Certainty

MANY COMMON QUESTIONS pertaining to Islamic law revolve around the issue of doubt. People will often ask questions like: "*what if* I feel like something came out", "the water *might* have some impurities", and "it *could* be that I prayed an extra unit". While these concerns usually arise out of well-meaning zeal, they can easily be resolved by understanding one principle that applies to all issues in Islamic law: doubt does not remove certainty. This means that when one is relatively sure about something, any doubts that arise in the mind should be discarded and not considered.

For example, if you have a doubt whether you have wuḍū' or not, go with what you are sure about. If you recall waking up from sleep and brushing your teeth, but do not remember whether or not you made wuḍū' then assume you do not have it. However, if you remember praying but do not recall whether or not you passed gas then assume you have it. In summary, if you doubt that you performed wuḍū', it must be performed. If you doubt that you broke it, it is assumed to be intact.

Another example is if you wake up and remember having an erotic dream but do not find any trace of semen on your clothes, you do not need to take a bath. You may ask yourself, "what if something came out but disappeared before I woke up?" The question is a legitimate one, but it is based on doubt rather than certainty. What is certain is that there are no perceptible traces of semen at all, and this certainty existed before you went to sleep. Therefore, the certainty is considered to remain intact and not overridden by doubts. It could only be overridden by another certainty such as if you saw the moisture of semen or smelled it on your clothes.

The same rule applies in determining exactly *when* something occurred. For example, if you completed your prayer and thirty minutes later notice that there is some impurity on your clothes, you may safely assume that it got on your clothes *after* the prayer. This assumption is valid as long as it is possible for it to have happened either before or after the prayer. However, if you were painting and then you performed wuḍū', prayed, and later found that you had paint on your hand, you must repeat the prayer if you did not come in contact with the paint after concluding the prayer. So the general rule is that when there are two equally likely times when an event might have occurred, you assume that it occurred later. However, if one of them is more likely, that should be given preference.

Appendix 2:

Difficulty Necessitates Ease

ONE PRINCIPLE that applies to all issues in Islamic law is that difficulty necessitates ease. This axiom means that whenever a person faces a very difficult circumstance, there is usually an exception to the rule. This may apply on an individual level where one who has difficulty standing for prayer may sit, lie down, or even pray in the heart. It may also apply on a societal level where people who live in areas where many birds fly overhead may consider the droppings from these birds to be pure.

Several common exceptions to the rule have already been mentioned in this book. However, it is important to note that when a person, or society, is faced with difficulty when trying to follow the guidance of Islam, there may be an exception to the rule to ease that difficulty. The best course of action is to ask a scholar specialized in the field of Islamic law whether or not an exception may apply. Never attempt to make exceptions yourself unless you are properly trained in the subject. This is because only an expert would know exactly how the exception should be made. For example, a person who is injured might know that there is an exception to the rule, but does it mean that the prayer can be skipped, delayed, or performed in a different way?

Bibliography

Books

Al-Ghunaymī, ʿAbd al-Ghanī, *al-Lubāb fī Sharḥ al-Kitāb* (Beirut: al-Maktabah al-ʿIlmiyyah, n.d.).

Ibn al-Fawzān, Ṣālīḥ, *Majmūʿ Fatāwā* (From *al-Maktabah al-Shamilah* [CD-ROM] 3.48).

Ibn al-Humām, al-Kamāl, *Fatḥ al-Qadīr* (Beirut: Dār al-Fikr, n.d.).

Ibn Rushd, Abul Walīd, *Bidāyah al-Mujtahid wa Nihāyah al-Muqtaṣid* (Cairo: Dārul Ḥadīth, 2004).

Ibn Taymiyyah, Taqī al-Dīn, *Majmūʿ al-Fatāwā* (Madinah: Majmaʿ al-Malik Fahd, 1995).

Al-Kāsānī, ʿAlā al-Dīn, *Badāiʿ al-Sanāi ʿfī Tartīb al-Sharāiʿ* (Beirut: Dār al-Kutub al-ʿIlmiyyah, 1986).

Mawlawī, Fayṣal, *Taysīr Fiqh al-ʿIbādāt* (Beirut: Mu'assassah al-Rayyān, 2001).

Al-Ṣābūnī, ʿMuḥammad Alī, *Fiqh al-ʿIbādāt* (Beirut: al-Maktabah al-ʿAsriyyah, 2007).

Al-Samarqandī, ʿAlā al-Dīn, *Tuḥfah al-Fuqahā'* (Beirut: Dār al-Kutub al-ʿIlmiyyah, 1994).

Al-Shāmī, Ibn ʿĀbidīn, *Radd al-Muḥtār* (Beirut: Dār al-Fikr, 1992).

Al-Shurunbulālī, Hasan, *Nur al-Idah: The Light of Clarification*, tr. Wesam Charkawi (UK: Azhar Academy Ltd, n.d.).

Websites

http://en.islamtoday.net/Fatwa-Archive

http://www.islamqa.com/enAskimam

http://www.daruliftaa.com

http://spa.qibla.com

http://www.dar-alifta.org

http://seekersguidance.org/ans-blog

http://www.zamzamacademy.com/view/fatawa

http://darulifta-deoband.org